THE BOOK OF
FLAGS

ROB COLSON

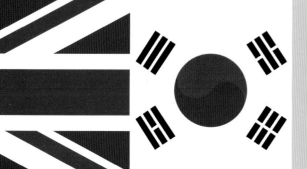

WAYLAND

CONTENTS

First published in Great Britain in 2016 by Wayland

Copyright © Wayland, 2016

All rights reserved

Editor: Julia Adams

Produced for Wayland by Tall Tree Ltd
Designer: Ben Ruocco

Dewey number: 929.9'2-dc23
ISBN (HB) 978 0 7502 9596 3
ISBN (PB) 978 0 7502 9828 5

Wayland, an imprint of Hachette Children's Group
Part of Hodder and Stoughton
Carmelite House
50 Victoria Embankment
London EC4Y 0DZ

An Hachette UK Company
www.hachette.co.uk
www.hachettechildrens.co.uk

Printed and bound in Malaysia

10 9 8 7 6 5 4 3 2 1

The publisher would like to thank the following for their kind
permission to reproduce their photographs:

Inside cover Pcheruvi/Dreamstime, 2 Hxdbzxy/Dreamstime,
5 britvich/Dreamstime, 7 NASA, 9 GBlakeley/istock, 13 Pruxo/CC,
17 Cylonphoto/Dreamstime, 29 Lornet/Dreamstime, 31 Davide
Romanini/Dreamstime, 35 duncan1890/istock, 36 Dmitry Berkut/
istock, 37 Sami Sert/istock, 39 Segafredo18/CC, 40 Grotmarsel/
istock, 45 Walter Dhladhla/AFP/Getty Images, 48 Gannet77/istock,
49 Jan Kranendonk/Dreamstime, 51 Nuvista/Dreamstime, 55 US
Airforce, 57 Janet Layher/Dreamstime, 59t snapgalleria/istock,
62 stevedangers/istock, 63 Ijacky/Dreamstime

Every attempt has been made to clear copyright. Should there be any
inadvertent omission, please apply to the publisher for rectification.

The website addresses (URLs) included in this book were valid at the
time of going to press. However, it is possible that contents
or addresses may have changed since the publication of this book.
No responsibility for any such changes can be accepted by either
the author or the Publisher.

PARTS OF A FLAG

Each part of a flag has a name. Here are some of the most important ones.

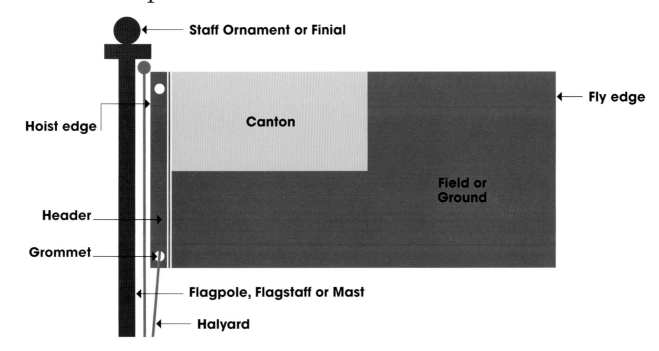

- Staff Ornament or Finial
- Fly edge
- Canton
- Hoist edge
- Field or Ground
- Header
- Grommet
- Flagpole, Flagstaff or Mast
- Halyard

TYPES OF FLAG

Flags are designed around a few basic patterns. These are some of the patterns that appear most frequently on national flags.

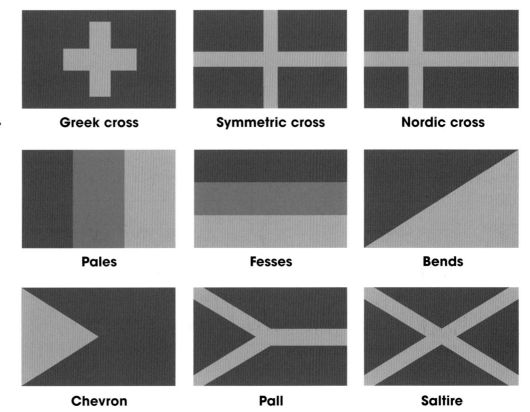

Greek cross	Symmetric cross	Nordic cross
Pales	Fesses	Bends
Chevron	Pall	Saltire

THE HISTORY OF FLAGS

We have used flags to signal to each other for thousands of years. We may be showing which country we belong to or which sports team we support, or we may be sending a warning or calling for help. Countries each have their own official flag. Many are instantly recognizable, and have become powerful symbols of the country's identity.

EARLY FLAGS

The earliest flags looked a little different from today's flags. They are called vexilloids (meaning 'flag-like'). In ancient Rome, vexilloids took the form of a cloth banner that was hung from a central staff. The banner would be carried into battle as a display of strength.

On the vexilloid of the Roman Empire were written the letters 'SPQR', standing for Senātus Populusque Rōmānus *(the Senate and People of Rome). At the top of the staff was a carved emblem of an eagle.*

HERALDRY

In medieval times, noble families devised designs that were painted on knights' shields or emblazoned on flags. These were called coats of arms. A complex set of meanings developed for the symbols used. The art of creating coats of arms out of these symbols is called heraldry.

Knights rode into battle wearing helmets that hid their faces. Their shields were decorated with their coat of arms to say which family they came from, and they would also carry banners that could be seen from long distance.

NAVAL FLAGS

Ships have long flown flags of various shapes and colours to identify themselves. In the 18th century, a system of flags was developed that allowed ships to signal to each other. Today, ships carry a set of signal flags, one for each letter in the alphabet, and ten more for the numbers 0–9.

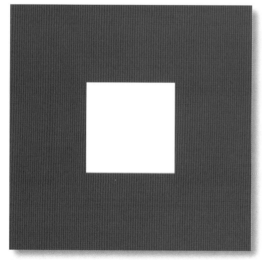

This flag, known as the Blue Peter, is a sign that you need to get on board as the ship is about to sail. It also stands for the letter 'P'.

The flag that is flown at the stern (back) of a ship to show its nationality is called an **ENSIGN**. It is often a different design from the national flag.

NATIONAL FLAGS

Flags to represent nations grew out of their previous use on battlefields or at sea. In the 18th century, various nationalist movements adopted flags to reinforce their sense of identity. Often the new national flags were based on the design of older battle flags. Today, every country has its own flag, whose design is normally fixed by special flag laws.

The driveway to the United Nations office in Geneva, Switzerland, is lined with the national flags of all 193 member states.

UNITED STATES OF AMERICA

The US flag has undergone many changes in its development. It is the symbol of the country's strength and unity and a prominent icon in national history.

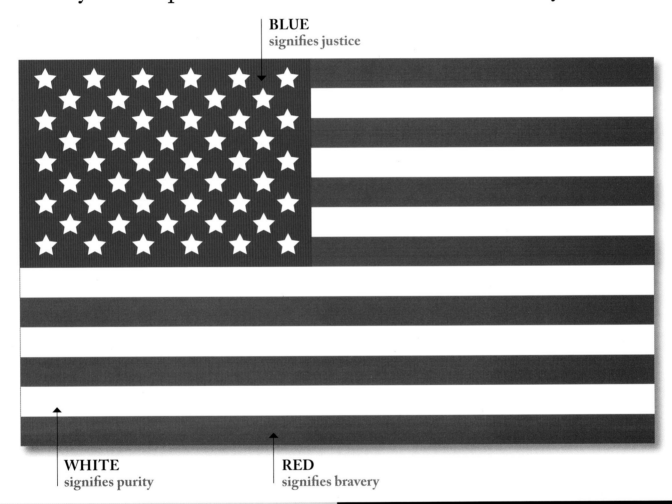

BLUE
signifies justice

WHITE
signifies purity

RED
signifies bravery

NAME:
The American flag, also called The Stars and Stripes, Red, White and Blue, The Star-Spangled Banner, and Old Glory.

DESIGN:
The 50 white stars of the American flag represent the 50 states of the USA, while the 13 red and white stripes stand for the 13 British colonies that declared independence from Great Britain in 1776.

US astronaut David R Scott salutes the American flag during the Apollo 15 *mission to the Moon in August 1971.*

FAST FLAG FACT

A 17-year-old schoolboy named Robert G Heft designed the current American flag for a school project, after Alaska and Hawaii became the 49th and 50th states in 1959. Astonishingly, he only scored a B minus for designing one of the world's most famous flags!

CONFEDERATE FLAG

The battle flag of the Confederacy, a group of slave-owning states that rebelled in the American Civl War, is still flown from some state buildings. To many, the flag symbolises racism against African Americans.

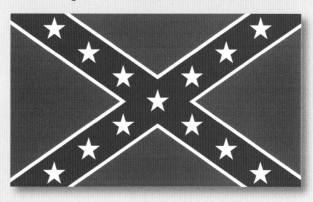

RECORD BREAKER

On 14 June 1992, Thomas Demski unveiled his 'Superflag', measuring 154 x 69 metres and weighing 1,350 kilograms! It takes 500 people to unfurl, has its own motor home to travel in and holds the world record for the world's largest flag.

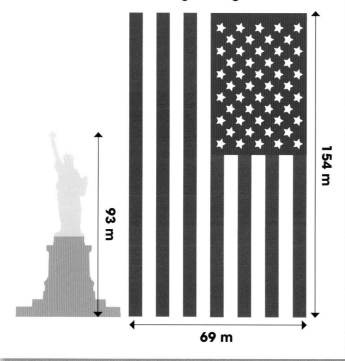

93 m

154 m

69 m

RAISING THE FLAG

Here are some of the special dates when the American flag should be flown at full staff:

1 January
New Year's Day

12 February
Presidents' Day

14 June
Flag Day

4 July
Independence Day

first Monday of September
Labor Day

fourth Thursday of November
Thanksgiving Day

CANADA

The national flag of Canada features a large red maple leaf at its centre. Maple trees grow all over the country and are a symbol of Canada. The maple leaf flag was first flown on 15 February 1965, which is now celebrated as National Flag Day.

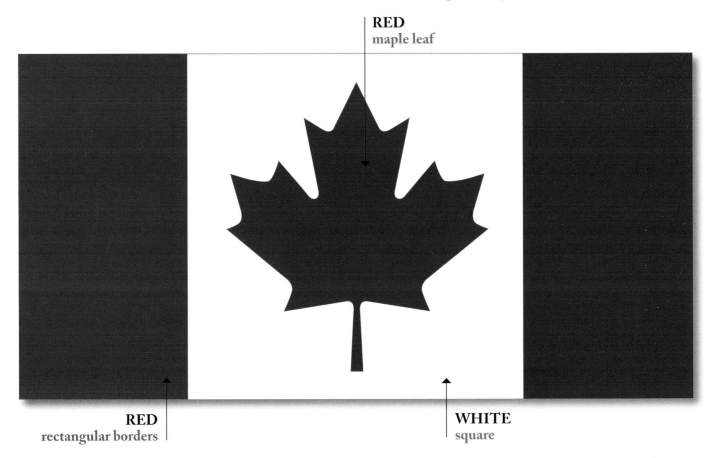

RED
maple leaf

RED
rectangular borders

WHITE
square

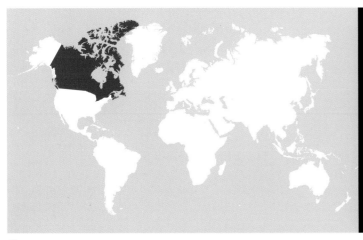

NAME:
National Flag of Canada, also called the Maple Leaf flag.

DESIGN:
A red 11-point leaf in a white square, with red rectangles on either side. The design was first proposed by Dr George Stanley, and was officially adopted in 1965. The leaf represents the ten different species of maple tree that grow across Canada.

PEACE TOWER

★★★

A Canadian national flag flies day and night at the top of the Peace Tower of the Canadian parliament in the capital city, Ottawa. The flag is changed for a new one every morning. Used flags are given away by the government, and the flags that have flown on the Peace Tower are the most highly prized. Anyone can apply for one, but there is a ten-year waiting list.

Each day a new flag is flown from the top of the Peace Tower.

FALLING LEAVES

Every autumn, the leaves of maple trees across Canada turn brilliant red or gold before falling to the ground. These falling leaves were first adopted as a symbol by French settlers around the St Lawrence River in the 18th century, in a region called New France. The leaves are now a symbol of the whole of Canada.

■ New France
■ English Colonies

St Lawrence River

RED ENSIGN

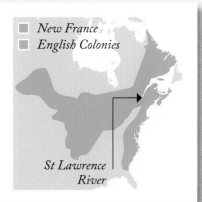

The shield also forms part of the Canadian royal coat of arms.

Before 1965, the Canadian Red Ensign was widely used as the national flag of Canada. It features a British Union Flag in the top left, showing that the country had been part of the British Empire. To the right is the shield of Canada, which features a sprig of three maple leaves at the bottom.

FAST FLAG FACT

The idea of a new flag was first put forward in 1964. There was disagreement in the Canadian House of Commons as some MPs wanted the Union Flag to be kept in the new design. Debate raged for more than six months before an agreement could be reached.

The clock tower sits at the centre of Canada's parliament buildings.

The shield that appears on some flags is called an **ESCUTCHEON**. The design on the escutcheon is called a **COAT OF ARMS**. The shape is taken from the shields used by medieval knights in battle.

BRAZIL

The Brazilian flag was adopted when the country became a republic in 1889. It replaced the flag of the Empire of Brazil, but kept its green background and gold diamond.

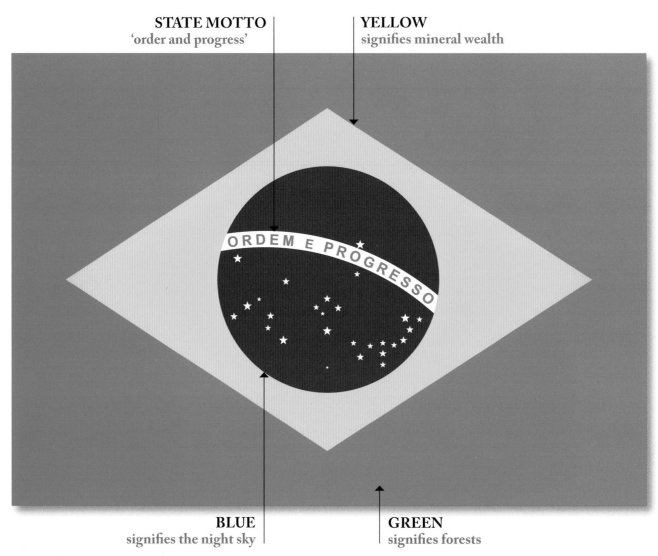

STATE MOTTO
'order and progress'

YELLOW
signifies mineral wealth

BLUE
signifies the night sky

GREEN
signifies forests

NAME:
The national flag of Brazil

DESIGN:
The flag was designed by Raimundo Teixeira Mendes. The 27 stars represent the 26 states of Brazil plus the federal district of the capital, Brazilia. In 1992, six stars were added after six new states had been created. The motto across the centre, 'Ordem e Progresso', means 'Order and Progress'.

CONSTELLATIONS

The stars are arranged to show the night sky as it was over Rio de Janeiro on 15 Novermber 1889, the day the flag was adopted. The star above the white band represents the one state in the Northern Hemisphere. Nine constellations are shown:

1. Procyon
2. Canis Major; five stars, the largest depicting Sirius.
3. Canopus
4. Spica
5. Hydra; two stars, the largest depicting Alphard.
6. Crux Australis; five stars, the largest depicting Alpha Crucis.
7. Sigma Octantis (south pole star).
8. Triangulum Australe; three stars of similar size.
9. Scorpius; eight stars,the largest depicting Antares.

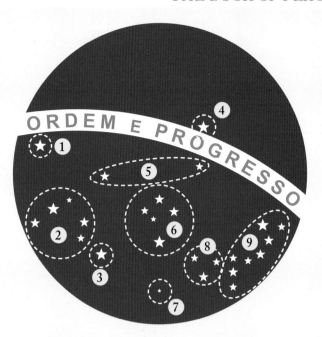

FOREST GREEN

More than half of the area of the Brazilian flag is coloured green. This represents the rainforests that cover nearly 60 per cent of the land.

Amazon Rainforest

FAMOUS KIT

Up to 1950, the Brazil national football team played in white shirts and shorts. Following a shock defeat to Uruguay in the 1950 World Cup final, the kit was changed to feature the colours of the national flag.

The emblem is the shield of the Brazil Football Federation. It also features the colours of the flag. The stars represent the five times Brazil have won the World Cup.

FAST FLAG FACT

So that flag makers can position the stars in the right place, the Brazilian government has produced an official construction sheet with the exact measurements on it. The gold diamond and blue circle must be a specific size, and the stars each have their own coordinates.

HALF-MAST describes a flag that is flying at least one flag-width down from the top of the pole. This is done to show a state of mourning when someone dies.

ARGENTINA

First adopted in 1812 during the war of independence with Spain, the Argentine flag symbolises the birth of a new nation. It was designed by Manuel Belgrano, a military leader in the war against Spain.

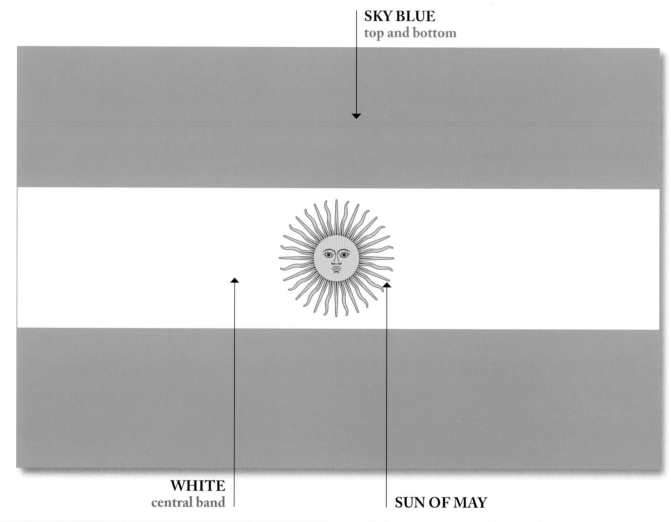

SKY BLUE
top and bottom

WHITE
central band

SUN OF MAY

NAME:
National Flag of Argentina

DESIGN:
Three equal horizontal bands. The middle band has a yellow Sun of May in its centre. The blue bands represent the sky and the River Plate, which runs through the capital city, Buenos Aires. The white represents silver, for which the region is famous – the name 'Argentina' means 'Land of Silver'.

THE SUN OF MAY

The emblem of a Sun with a human face appears both on the Argentine flag and on the flag of neighbouring Uruguay. It is called the Sun of May after the May Revolution of 1810 that started the war of independence. The emblem was designed by Juan de Dios Rivera Túpac, a descendant of a royal Inca family, and pays tribute to the Inca Sun god Inti.

On the Uruguayan flag, the Sun has 8 wavy sunbeams and 8 straight ones.

On the Argentinian flag, the Sun has 16 wavy sunbeams and 16 straight ones.

PRESIDENTIAL SASH

At official functions, the presidents of many countries wear a presidential sash. This is a piece of cloth in the colours of the national flag that is worn over the right shoulder.

When a president leaves office, the sash is handed over to the new president at an official ceremony.

The first coin to be minted for the new country of Argentina, in 1813, featured the Sun of May on one side.

FAST FLAG FACT

The anniversary of the death of Manuel Belgrano, 20 June, is a public holiday in Argentina called National Flag Day. Each year on this day, the people of the city of Rosario carry an Argentine flag in a public parade. The flag is hundreds of metres long.

The **TRIBAND**, a flag with three stripes of equal size, is the most popular design for national flags. The stripes can run either horizontally or vertically.

JAMAICA

The flag of Jamaica was adopted on 6 August 1962, the day that Jamaica gained independence from the United Kingdom. It features a gold saltire (cross) and green and black triangles.

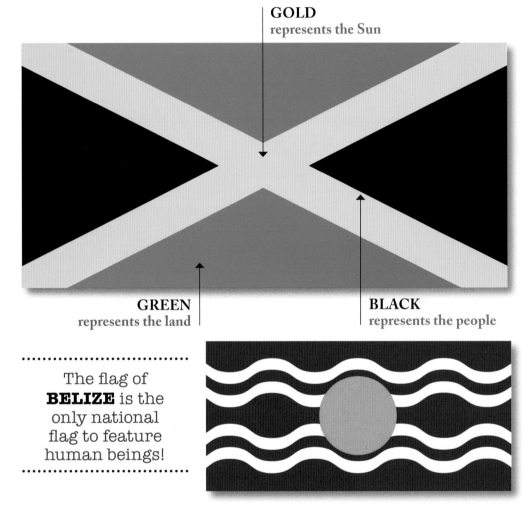

GOLD
represents the Sun

GREEN
represents the land

BLACK
represents the people

WEST INDIES FEDERATION

From 1958 to 1962, Jamaica belonged to the British West Indies Federation, an association of colonies that planned to gain independence as one unified state. The federation collapsed and nine separate independent states were formed instead. The West Indies Federation flag (left) symbolised the Sun over the Caribbean Sea.

The flag of **BELIZE** is the only national flag to feature human beings!

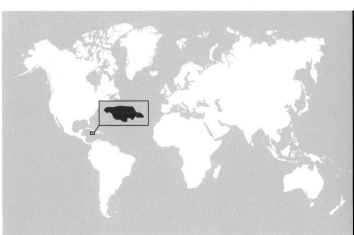

NAME:
The Jamaica National Flag

DESIGN:
The design emerged from a public competition. Gold represents the Sun, green represents the fertile land, and black represents the strength and creativity of the people.

CUBA

The national flag of Cuba was first raised on 20 May 1902 to mark the island's independence from Spain. The colours and design are partly inspired by the flag of the USA.

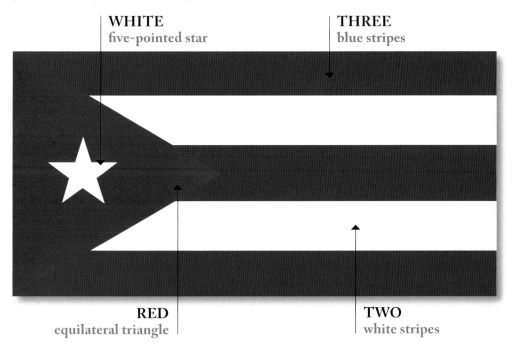

WHITE
five-pointed star

THREE
blue stripes

RED
equilateral triangle

TWO
white stripes

A **CHEVRON** is a 'V'-shaped pattern that appears on flags and on military and police uniforms.

The flag of the 26 July Movement features the date written against a red and black background.

26 JULY MOVEMENT

Many of Cuba's national holidays celebrate the country's revolutionary past. Revolution Day on 26 July marks the 1959 revolution that brought Fidel Castro to power. The revolutionaries called themselves the 26 July Movement, after the day of an attack by Castro's forces on the Moncada Barracks in Santiago de Cuba in 1953.

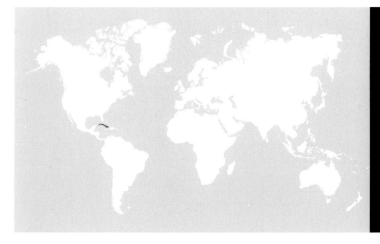

NAME:
The National Flag of Cuba, also known as The Lone Star flag

DESIGN:
The flag was designed in 1850 by the Venezuelan Narciso López, who fought against Spanish rule in Cuba. The blue stripes represent the three departments into which Cuba was divided. The single star may represent López's desire for Cuba to become part of the USA.

INTERNATIONAL FLAGS

Many international organisations have their own flags, which symbolise the unity of the nations that belong to the organisation.

OLIVE BRANCHES
symbolise peace

SIX CONTINENTS
represent the member states

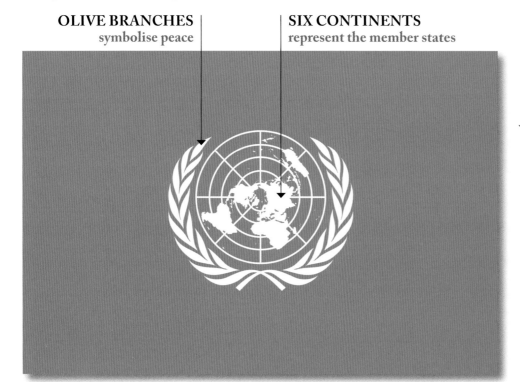

UNITED NATIONS
★ ★ ★ ★ ★ ★ ★ ★ ★ ★ ★ ★ ★

The flag of the United Nations shows a map of the world centred on the North Pole, cradled by two olive branches. The organisation was formed on 24 October 1945, at the end of World War II, to promote international cooperation. The olive branches represent peace between nations.

FLAG OF EUROPE
★ ★ ★ ★ ★ ★ ★ ★ ★ ★ ★ ★ ★

The Flag of Europe is the flag of the European Union, an organisation of 28 European states. Its design of 12 yellow stars on a blue background was inspired by the halo of 12 stars that the Virgin Mary is said to have worn in the Bible.

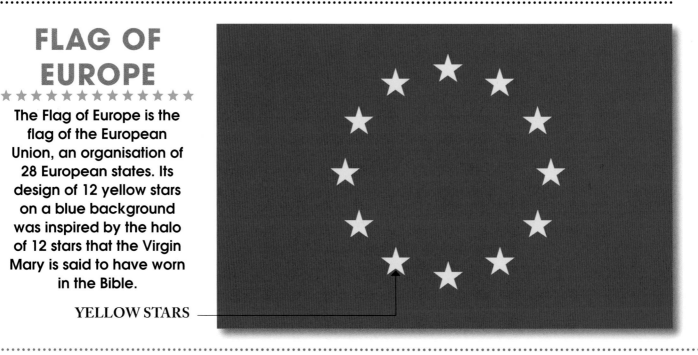

YELLOW STARS

INTERNATIONAL RED CROSS AND RED CRESCENT

★ ★

The Red Cross and Red Crescent are international movements that provide emergency medical services in crisis areas. They often do very dangerous work in war zones, and their distinctive flags are clearly emblazoned on their vehicles and equipment. This tells others not to fire on them.

Distinctive symbol stands out clearly.

AFRICAN UNION

The African Union is an organization that includes every African country except Morocco. Its flag features an outline of Africa surrounded by 54 gold stars – one for each member state.

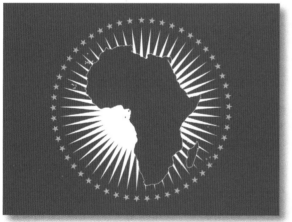

National flags at the United Nations are always flown in **ALPHABETICAL ORDER**. This ensures that no country's flag is ever thought of as more important.

NATO

★ ★

The North Atlantic Treaty Organisation (NATO) was formed in 1949 as a military alliance between the USA, Canada and countries in western Europe to counter the threat that they felt from the Soviet Union. It has since grown to include most of Europe and Turkey. The deep blue background symbolises the Atlantic Ocean. In the centre is a compass rose that points North, South, East and West. The circle around the rose symbolises unity.

FAST FLAG FACT

Nobody knows who first came up with the design for the emblem that appears on the NATO flag. It was probably designed by a member of the organization's International Staff. The flag was officially approved in 1953.

PORTUGAL

The flag of Portugal was adopted in 1911, a year after the country was declared a republic. The flag celebrates Portugal's maritime past.

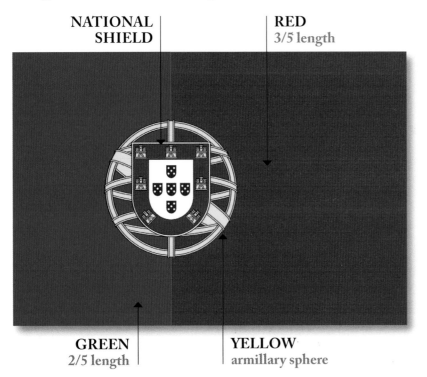

NATIONAL SHIELD

RED 3/5 length

GREEN 2/5 length

YELLOW armillary sphere

FAST FLAG FACT

The shield celebrates the victory of King Afonso Henriques I over the Moors in the 12th century. The five blue shields and seven golden castles represent the defeated Moorish kings and their strongholds.

NATION OF EXPLORERS

The flag features an armillary sphere, an instrument used to model the earth and heavens in medieval times. The sphere was first adopted as a Portuguese emblem in the 15th century by King Manuel I, and reflected the prowess of Portuguese sailors and explorers at the time, who were establishing a vast Portuguese empire around the world.

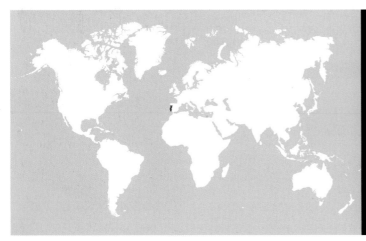

NAME:
The flag of Portugal

DESIGN:
A vertical red band next to a wider green band, with the national shield sitting inside an armillary sphere, half on the red and half on the green. The red band is 1.5 times the width of the green band.

SPAIN

The current version of the Spanish flag dates from 1981, but the distinctive red-and-gold colours have symbolised Spain ever since they were chosen by King Carlos III in 1785.

COAT OF ARMS
height is 2/5 flag height

YELLOW
central stripe (also called 'gualda')

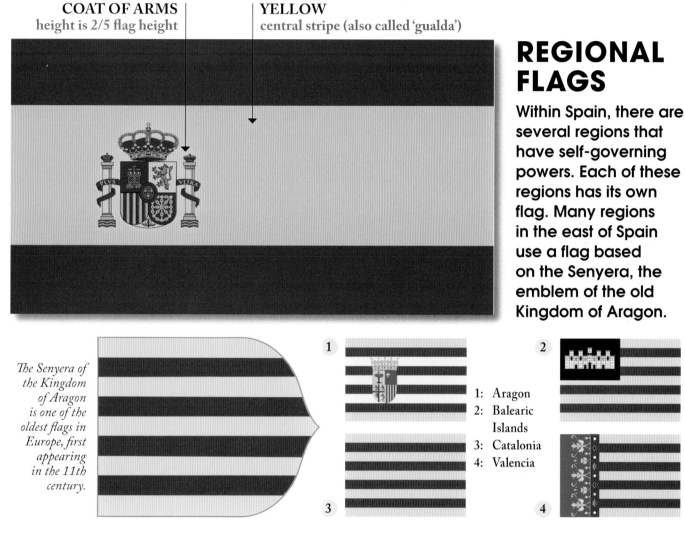

The Senyera of the Kingdom of Aragon is one of the oldest flags in Europe, first appearing in the 11th century.

1: Aragon
2: Balearic Islands
3: Catalonia
4: Valencia

REGIONAL FLAGS

Within Spain, there are several regions that have self-governing powers. Each of these regions has its own flag. Many regions in the east of Spain use a flag based on the Senyera, the emblem of the old Kingdom of Aragon.

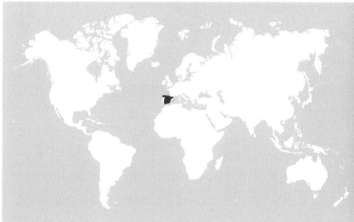

NAME:
Flag of Spain, also known as the 'Rojigualda' (meaning red and gold)

DESIGN:
A stripe of yellow between two horizontal red stripes. In the yellow stripe, nearer to the hoist edge, is the Spanish coat of arms. Sometimes the coat of arms is left off the flag. The original design was made by naval officer Antonio Valdés y Fernández Bazán.

GERMANY

The black, red and gold tricolour first appeared as the flag of the Confederation of German states in 1848. It was adopted as the national flag of Germany in 1919. The flag sometimes appears with the German coat of arms at the centre.

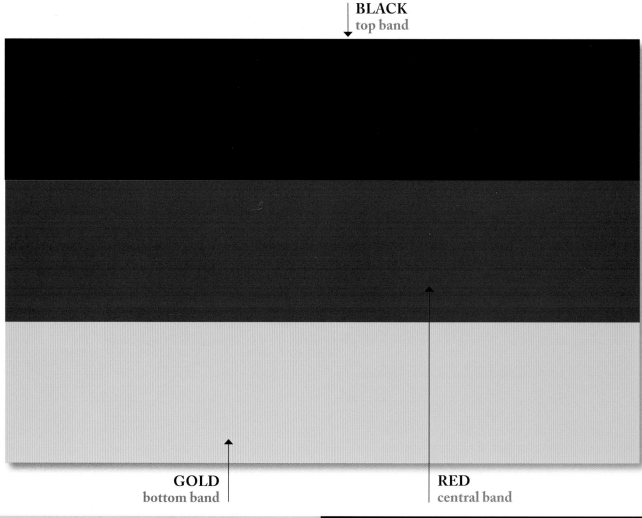

BLACK
top band

GOLD
bottom band

RED
central band

NAME:
The Federal Flag

DESIGN:
Three equal horizontal bands with black at the top, red in the middle and gold at the bottom. The width to length ratio is 3:5.

BLACK EAGLE

The colours of the German flag are taken from the banner for the Holy Roman Empire, an alliance of kingdoms that covered much of central Europe from 962 to 1806. The banner featured a black eagle with red claws and beak on a gold background. The official German coat of arms has the same design.

GERMANY DIVIDED

At the end of World War II, the Nazis were defeated and Germany was divided into two countries: the capitalist Federal Republic (West Germany) and the communist Democratic Republic (East Germany). At first, both countries had the same flag, but in 1959, East Germany added a new emblem. It showed a hammer and compass surrounded by a ring of rye, representing work, education and farming. Germany was reunited in 1990.

East Germany's emblem reflected its communist government's ideals.

NAZI FLAG

★ ★ ★ ★ ★ ★ ★ ★ ★

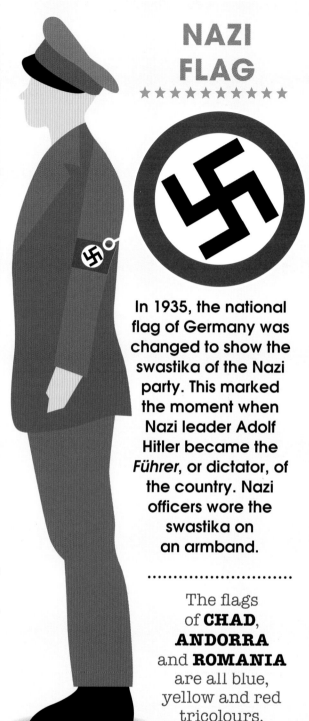

In 1935, the national flag of Germany was changed to show the swastika of the Nazi party. This marked the moment when Nazi leader Adolf Hitler became the *Führer*, or dictator, of the country. Nazi officers wore the swastika on an armband.

....

The flags of **CHAD**, **ANDORRA** and **ROMANIA** are all blue, yellow and red tricolours.

....

FAST FLAG FACT

The German state flag includes the German coat of arms at its centre. This flag can only be flown by official government authorities. The plain tricolour is known as the civil flag, and can be flown by anybody who wishes to fly it.

THE UNITED KINGDOM

The Flag of the United Kingdom of Great Britain and Northern Ireland combines three different flags to represent the kingdoms that were united to form the single state of the UK.

BLUE
for Scotland

RED
cross for Ireland

RED
cross for England

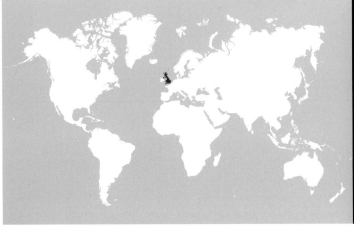

NAME:
The Union Flag, or the Union Jack

DESIGN:
The Cross of St George above the Cross of St Andrew and the Cross of St Patrick.

St Andrew's Cross + St George's Cross = Great Union Flag

+

St Patrick's Cross

=

Union Flag

THE MAKING OF THE UNION JACK

★★★★★★★★★★★★★★★★★★★★★★★★★★★★★★★★★

The first Union Flag was officially adopted in 1707 with the union of the Kingdoms of England and Scotland to form the Kingdom of Great Britain. The new flag combined the flags of Scotland and England. In 1801, Ireland was united with Britain, and the flag of Great Britain was combined with the flag of Ireland to form today's Union Flag.

Quarters of a flag are called **CANTONS**. The flags of some former British colonies such as Australia have the Union Flag in the upper hoist canton.

WELSH DRAGON

While England, Scotland and Ireland are represented on the flag, Wales is not. This is because Wales was already part of the English Kingdom when England united with Scotland. Wales has its own flag, with a red dragon on a white and green background.

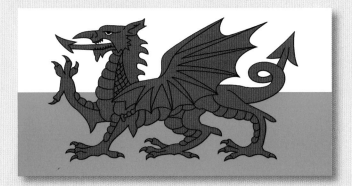

REPUBLIC OF IRELAND

In 1922, following the Irish War of Independence, the Irish Free State left the United Kingdom to form an independent country. The new state adopted a new flag with green, white and orange bands. In 1937, it became the Republic of Ireland. Six counties in the north of Ireland remained in the UK, becoming the separate province of Northern Ireland.

FRANCE

The red, white and blue tricolour was adopted as the French national flag in 1894. This took place during the French Revolution, which swept the old monarchy out of power.

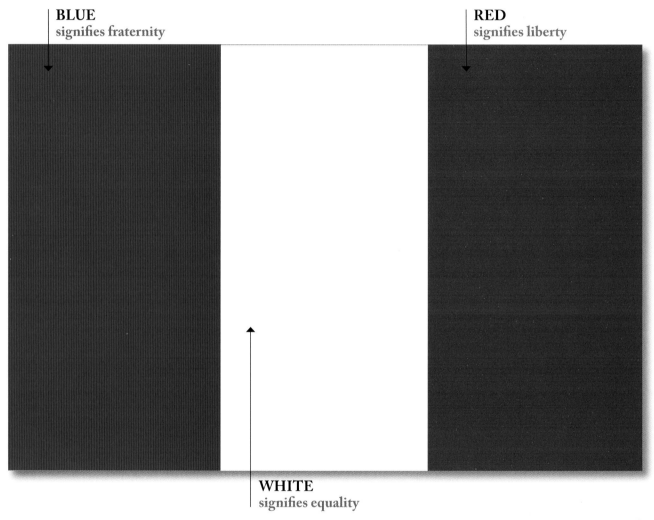

BLUE
signifies fraternity

RED
signifies liberty

WHITE
signifies equality

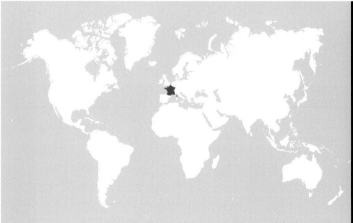

NAME:
The tricolour (meaning three colours)

DESIGN:
Three vertical bands of equal width, coloured blue, white and red, with the blue band nearest to the flagstaff. Originally, the colours represented the monarchy and the city of Paris, but they have since come to represent the national motto of France: 'Liberty, Equality and Fraternity'.

AIRCRAFT ROUNDEL

★★★★★★★★★★★★★★★★★★★★★★★

During World War I, the French air force painted a circular version of the tricolour, called a roundel, on the sides of their planes. This allowed allies to identify them and avoid shooting them down by mistake. Other countries' air forces soon followed suit with circular versions of their own flags. The roundel was easier to spot than a regular flag shape.

FAST FLAG FACT

Since the 16th century, the tricolour flag has been associated with republics – countries without a royal family. Today, 15 countries have flags with three equal vertical stripes, many of them inspired by the French Tricolour.

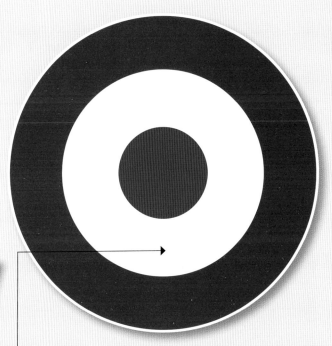

Roundels are painted on both sides of the wings and on each side of the fuselage so that they can be seen from any angle.

ROYAL LILY

Before the French Revolution, the symbol of France was the fleur-de-lis, a stylised lily flower. This design was associated with the French royal family, the House of Bourbon, who were overthrown during the Revolution. The French king, Louis XVI, was executed in 1893, and the new flag represented the end of the old monarchy.

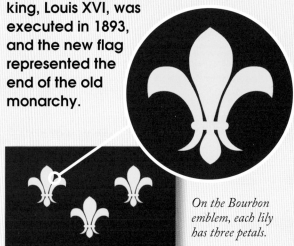

On the Bourbon emblem, each lily has three petals.

FREE FRENCH FORCES

During World War II, France was occupied by Germany from 1940 to 1944. Forces fighting the occupation adopted a new flag to represent the Free French State. It was the tricolour with a Cross of Lorraine in the centre. The Cross of Lorraine, also known as the Crusader's Cross, was used by the Knights Templar during the Christian Crusades between the 11th and 13th centuries.

The flag of the principality of **MONACO** uses the same red and white colours as the flag of Indonesia. Monaco's flag is a little narrower.

DENMARK

The white Nordic cross on a red background was officially adopted as the national flag of Denmark in 1748, but various versions of the cross date back to 1400.

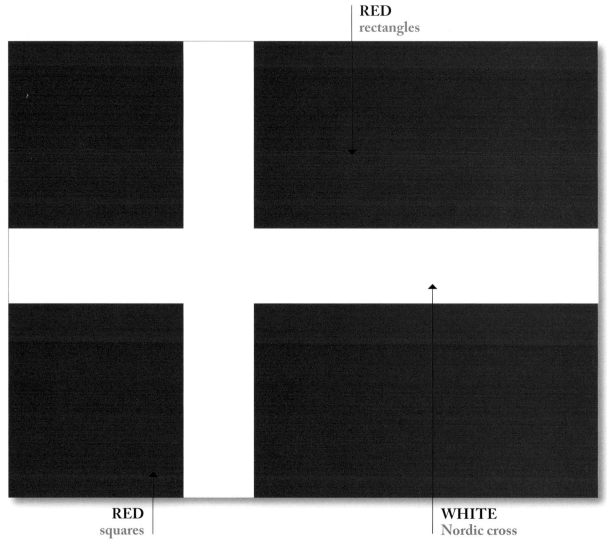

RED
rectangles

RED
squares

WHITE
Nordic cross

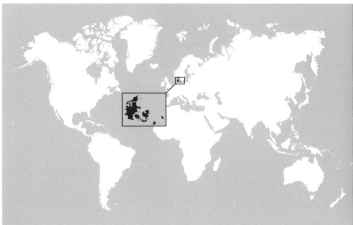

NAME:
Dannebrog
('the flag of the Danes' or 'the red flag')

DESIGN:
A white cross on a red background. The cross is offset towards the hoist side, dividing the background into two squares to the hoist side and two rectangles to the fly side.

NORDIC CROSS

★★★★★★★★★★★★★★★★★★★★★★★★★

Every country in Scandinavia has a flag with a Nordic cross, and it is also used for the flags of the British Orkney and Shetland Islands. The design is inspired by the Christian cross, and was first used during the Crusades in the Middle Ages.

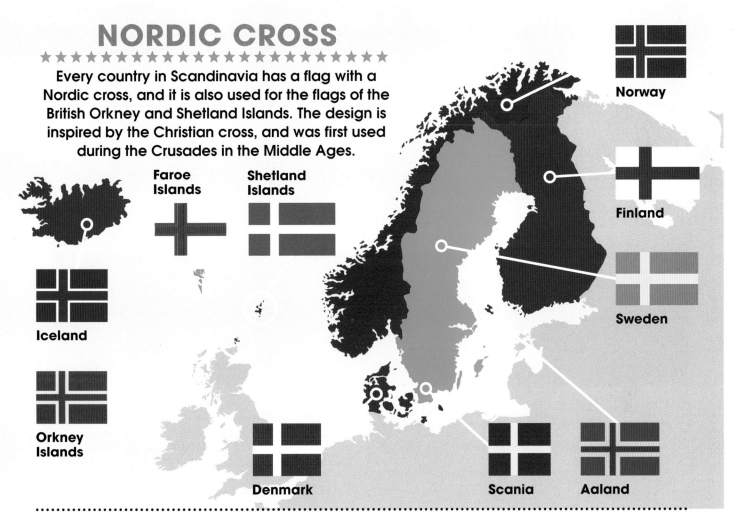

Faroe Islands

Shetland Islands

Iceland

Orkney Islands

Denmark

Norway

Finland

Sweden

Scania

Aaland

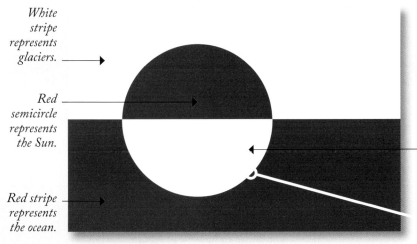

White stripe represents glaciers.

Red semicircle represents the Sun.

Red stripe represents the ocean.

White semicircle represents the underwater part of an iceberg.

When it enters a port, a ship will often fly the flag of the country it is visiting. This is known as a **COURTESY FLAG**.

GREENLAND

The island of Greenland off the coast of North America has been a Danish colony since 1814. Today, it has a great deal of independence, and the Greenland flag is flown alongside the Danish flag on official buildings. The white stripe represents the glaciers that cover most of the island, while the red stripe is the ocean. The red semicircle is the Sun on the horizon, and the white semicircle is an iceberg. The colours are the same as those on the Danish flag.

THE NETHERLANDS

The flag of the Netherlands was officially made the national flag in 1937, but it had been in use since 1572, making it possibly the oldest tricolour flag in the world.

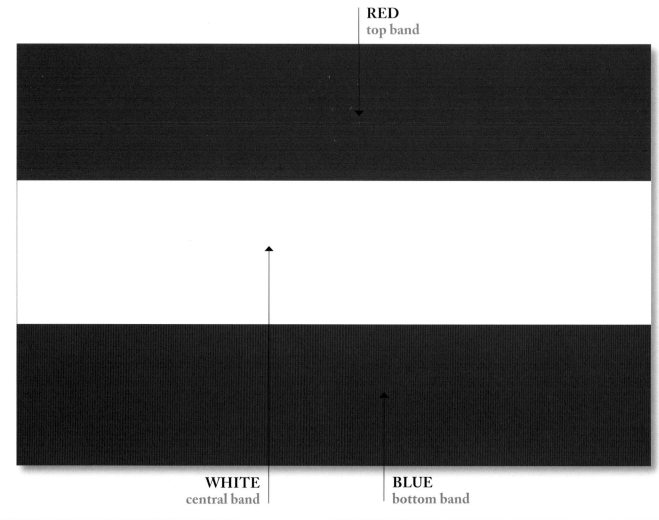

RED
top band

WHITE
central band

BLUE
bottom band

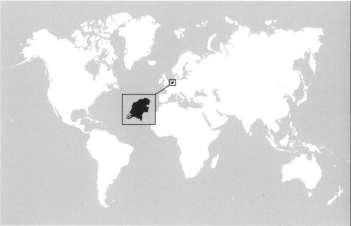

NAME:
National flag of the Netherlands

DESIGN:
Three horizontal bands of equal size, with red at the top, white in the middle and blue at the bottom.

NEW YORK CITY

The flag of New York City features the flag of the Dutch Republic, which founded the city as New Amsterdam on the southern tip of Manhattan Island in 1625. Forty years later, the British captured the settlement and renamed it New York. In the middle of the flag is the seal of the city. The flag flies above New York City Hall and other official buildings.

Seal of the city features a European sailor and a member of the Lenape tribe.

NAVAL JACK

The Dutch Naval Jack is the flag flown by ships in the Royal Netherlands Navy. Lines from the centre divide the flag into triangles, which carry the colours of the national flag. This design is called a gironny.

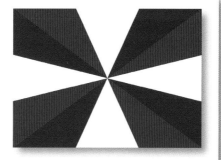

A **PENNANT**, or **PENNON**, is a narrow flag with a pointed or forked end that is often flown on ships.

ROYAL ORANGE

On the King's Day, the orange royal pennant is flown with the national flag.

The colour most associated with the Netherlands is not found on the flag. The Dutch royal family belong to the House of Orange-Nassau, which has reigned since 1815. Every year, people across the Netherlands wear orange to celebrate the King's Day. The Dutch flag is flown with an orange penant next to it.

ITALY

The green, white and red tricolour was officially adopted as the national flag of Italy in 1948, when the modern Italian Republic was formed.

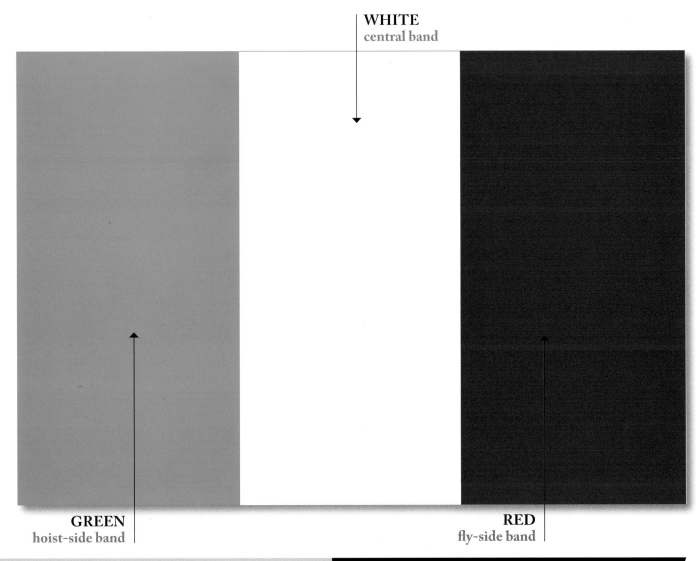

WHITE
central band

GREEN
hoist-side band

RED
fly-side band

NAME:
Il tricolore (the tricolour)

DESIGN:
Three vertical bands, with green at the hoist side, white in the middle and red at the fly side. The three-colour design was originally inspired by the French flag.

The statue of Garibaldi in Genoa is draped with a red cape on special occasions.

ITALIAN UNIFICATION

★ ★

In the 19th century, Italy was divided into different states. The states united to form the Kingdom of Italy in 1871, following a series of conflicts known as the Risorgimiento. Giussseppe Garibaldi was an important figure in the Risorgimiento, leading many daring military campaigns. His soldiers could not afford uniforms so they all made sure that they were wearing red. They came to be known as the Redshirts.

FAST FLAG FACT

Flying a flag upside-down is an international signal of distress, meaning that you need help. Often the flag will have a knot tied in it at the fly side before turning it round to make the signal clearer.

VATICAN CITY

In the centre of the city of Rome is the smallest independent state in the world. It is called Vatican City, and is a walled-off area covering just 44 hectares. Vatican City is the home of the Bishop of Rome, also known as the Pope. Up to 1870, the Pope ruled over an area of central Italy called the Papal States. After the unification of Italy, this was reduced to just the area within Vatican City.

The coat of arms of Vatican City appears on its flag. It features a gold key crossed over a silver key, symbolising the keys of St Peter.

FOOD OF THE FLAG

Italian chefs have invented many different ways to represent the national colours in their food. A popular starter is a tricolore salad, made from avocado, mozzarella cheese and tomatoes. Follow that up with a tricolore pasta dish, with spinach pasta, egg pasta and tomato pasta. Then finish off your meal with a tricolore ice cream mix of mint, vanilla and strawberry flavours.

BALKAN STATES

The region surrounding the Balkan Mountains in southeast Europe is home to people of diverse cultures and religions. The Balkans have had a turbulent recent history, and many new states have emerged following years of conflict.

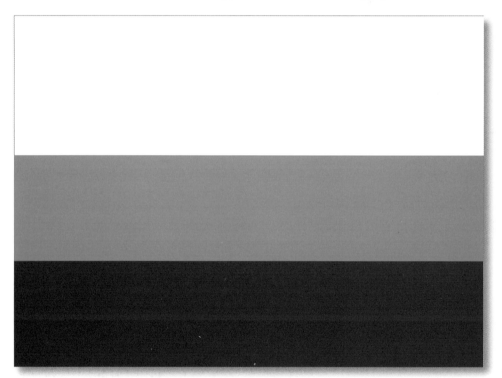

BULGARIA

★ ★ ★ ★ ★ ★ ★ ★ ★ ★ ★ ★

Bulgaria adopted the white, green and red tricolour when it gained independence within the Ottoman Empire in 1878. The country became fully independent in 1908. Socialist symbols were added to the flag during communist rule after World War II. These were removed in 1990 when the communist regime collapsed.

The Bulgarian flag has no fixed width-to-length ratio.

GREECE

★ ★ ★ ★ ★ ★ ★ ★ ★ ★ ★ ★ ★ ★

The Greek national flag was officially adopted in 1978. The cross in the top corner symbolises Greek Orthodox Christianity. Next to the cross are nine stripes of alternating blue and white. Many theories exist as to the meaning of the stripes. Some say that they represent the nine Muses of ancient Greek mythology – goddesses who were thought to be the source of all knowledge.

Unlike most national flags, the shade of the Greek flag's colours is not specified, and any shade of blue is allowed.

Afghanistan | Angola | Albania | Algeria | Andorra | Antigua and Barbuda | Argentina | Armenia

Belgium | Belize | Benin | Bhutan | Bolivia | Bosnia and Herzegovina | Botswana | Brazil

Cape Verde | Central African Republic | Chad | Chile | China | Colombia | Comoros | Congo

DR Congo | East Timor | Ecuador | Egypt | El Salvador | Equatorial Guinea | Eritrea | Estonia

Ghana | Greece | Grenada | Guatemala | Guinea Bissau | Guinea | Guyana | Haiti

Ireland | Israel | Italy | Ivory Coast | Jamaica | Japan | Jordan | Kazakhstan

Lesotho | Liberia | Libya | Liechtenstein | Lithuania | Luxembourg | Macedonia | Madagascar

Mexico | Micronesia | Mongolia | Moldova | Monaco | Montenegro | Morocco | Mozambique

North Korea | Norway | Oman | Pakistan | Palau | Panama | Papua New Guinea | Paraguay

St Kitts and Nevis | St Lucia | St Vincent - Grenadines | Samoa | San Marino | Sao Tome and Principe | Saudi Arabia | Senegal

South Africa | South Korea | South Sudan | Spain | Sri Lanka | Sudan | Suriname | Swaziland

Trinidad and Tobago | Tunisia | Turkey | Turkmenistan | Tuvalu | Thailand | Uganda | Ukraine

Yemen | Zambia | Zimbabwe | Roman Empire | US Confederacy | Canadian Red Ensign | West Indies Confederation | 26 July Movement

Holy Roman Empire | St Andrew's Cross | St George's Cross | Great Union | St Patrick's Cross | Wales | Free French State | House of Bourbon

Yugoslavia | USSR | Kurdistan | Socialist Red | LGBTQ Pride | Anarchist | African National Congress | Apartheid South Africa

Shark alert | Get out of the water | Jolly Roger | Macau | Hong Kong | Joseon Kingdom | Imperial Japanese Army | Thai elephant

Slippery track | Return to pit lane | Driver warning | Driver disqualification | Safety car deployment | Let car behind overtake | Assistant referee | Greek cross

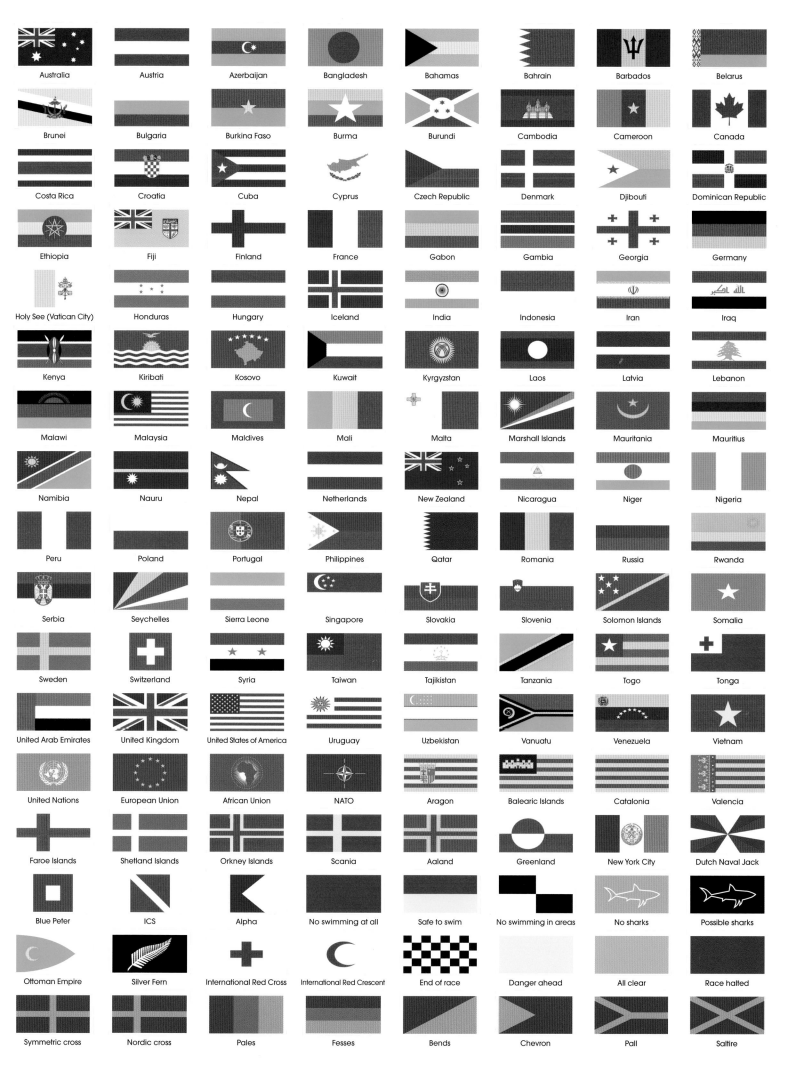

Australia	Austria	Azerbaijan	Bangladesh	Bahamas	Bahrain	Barbados	Belarus
Brunei	Bulgaria	Burkina Faso	Burma	Burundi	Cambodia	Cameroon	Canada
Costa Rica	Croatia	Cuba	Cyprus	Czech Republic	Denmark	Djibouti	Dominican Republic
Ethiopia	Fiji	Finland	France	Gabon	Gambia	Georgia	Germany
Holy See (Vatican City)	Honduras	Hungary	Iceland	India	Indonesia	Iran	Iraq
Kenya	Kiribati	Kosovo	Kuwait	Kyrgyzstan	Laos	Latvia	Lebanon
Malawi	Malaysia	Maldives	Mali	Malta	Marshall Islands	Mauritania	Mauritius
Namibia	Nauru	Nepal	Netherlands	New Zealand	Nicaragua	Niger	Nigeria
Peru	Poland	Portugal	Philippines	Qatar	Romania	Russia	Rwanda
Serbia	Seychelles	Sierra Leone	Singapore	Slovakia	Slovenia	Solomon Islands	Somalia
Sweden	Switzerland	Syria	Taiwan	Tajikistan	Tanzania	Togo	Tonga
United Arab Emirates	United Kingdom	United States of America	Uruguay	Uzbekistan	Vanuatu	Venezuela	Vietnam
United Nations	European Union	African Union	NATO	Aragon	Balearic Islands	Catalonia	Valencia
Faroe Islands	Shetland Islands	Orkney Islands	Scania	Aaland	Greenland	New York City	Dutch Naval Jack
Blue Peter	ICS	Alpha	No swimming at all	Safe to swim	No swimming in areas	No sharks	Possible sharks
Ottoman Empire	Silver Fern	International Red Cross	International Red Crescent	End of race	Danger ahead	All clear	Race halted
Symmetric cross	Nordic cross	Pales	Fesses	Bends	Chevron	Pall	Saltire

YUGOSLAVIA

★ ★

Between 1922 and 1991, Yugoslavia was the largest country in the Balkans. It became a socialist federation in 1946, made up of six autonomous republics. The flag of the Socialist Federal Republic of Yugoslavia added a red star to the blue, white and red of the Kingdom of Yugoslavia that it replaced.

BREAK-UP OF YUGOSLAVIA

In the 1980s, tensions rose between the republics of Yugoslavia, and a series of wars broke out in 1991. By 2006, Yugoslavia had split into six officially recognised countries. An ongoing dispute exists over a seventh region, Kosovo, which is recognised as a separate country by only part of the international community.

Narrow lines of colour are sometimes used on a flag to make the design stand out more clearly. This is called called **FIMBRIATION**.

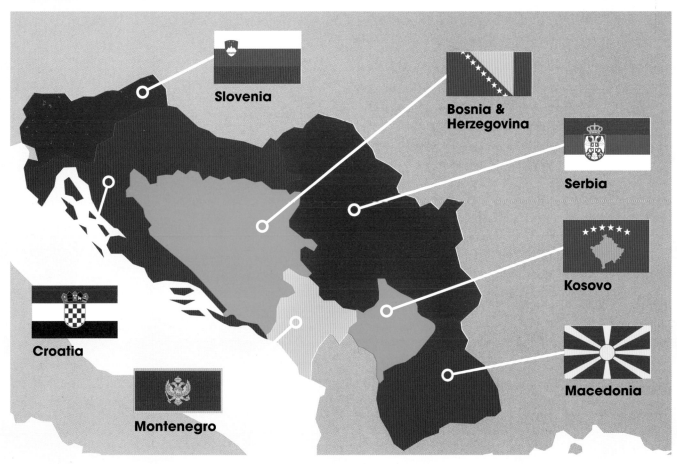

Slovenia

Bosnia & Herzegovina

Serbia

Kosovo

Croatia

Montenegro

Macedonia

RUSSIA

The white, blue and red tricolour has been the flag of the Russian Federation since 1991. It was first used more than 300 years ago by Peter the Great, and had been the official flag of Tsarist Russia before the Russian Revolution of 1917.

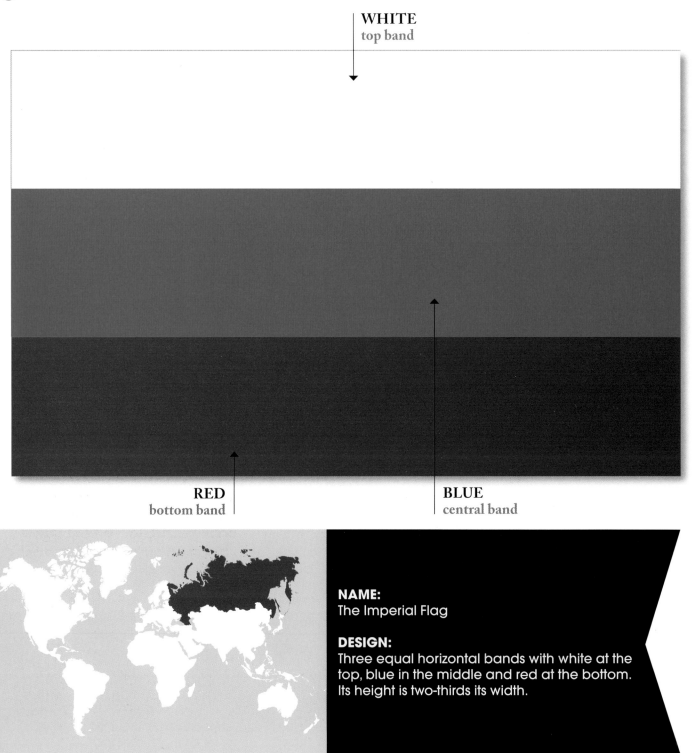

WHITE
top band

RED
bottom band

BLUE
central band

NAME:
The Imperial Flag

DESIGN:
Three equal horizontal bands with white at the top, blue in the middle and red at the bottom. Its height is two-thirds its width.

THE SOVIET ERA

Following the Bolshevik Revolution of 1917, Russia became the largest state in the Union of Soviet Socialist Republics (USSR). The flag of the USSR had a red background, with a hammer and a sickle in the corner to symbolise workers and peasants, plus a star to symbolise socialism. The design was the result of a competition held in 1917. The hammer and sickle symbol has since been used by communist groups across the world.

The background of the Soviet flag was changed to a brighter red in its final version, dating from 1980.

Peter the Great (above) ruled Russia from 1682 to 1725. He expanded the empire and turned Russia into a major power. The country returned to Peter's flag when the Soviet Union fell.

Founded in 1923, the Soviet airline Aeroflot added wings to the hammer and sickle for its logo.

FAST FLAG FACT

Tsar Peter the Great visited the Netherlands in 1697 to study their shipbuilding methods. It is said that he was impressed by the simple design of the Dutch flag, and used it as the basis for his own flag.

KAZAKHSTAN

Since the end of the USSR in 1991, many of the former Soviet republics have become independent states. Kazakhstan is the largest of these new states. Its flag is based on a design by Kazakh artist Shaken Niyazbekov, and shows the Sun with a golden steppe eagle underneath it, on a sky blue background. To the hoist side is a pattern called *koshkar-muiz* (the horns of a ram).

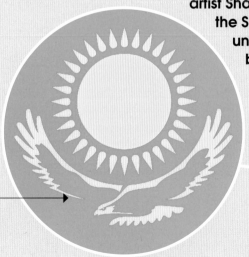

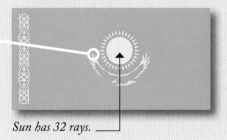

The steppe eagle is seen in Kazakh skies during summer. In winter it heads south to warmer places such as North Africa.

Sun has 32 rays.

POLITICAL FLAGS

Many political movements adopt flags to represent the ideals they stand for. The images they choose often come to strongly symbolise particular political positions.

The Sun at the centre of the flag has 21 rays. The number 21 is an important in the Ezidi religion practised by many Kurds.

KURDISTAN
★ ★ ★ ★ ★ ★ ★ ★ ★ ★ ★ ★ ★ ★

Nationalist movements often have their own flags, which they hope will one day become the national flag of a new country. Kurdish nationalists fight for an independent state for the Kurdish people, who today live in parts of Iraq, Syria, Iran and Turkey. The new state would be called Kurdistan, and its flag would be the current flag of the Kurdish part of Iraq.

SOCIALIST RED
★ ★ ★ ★ ★ ★ ★ ★ ★ ★ ★ ★ ★ ★ ★ ★

During a series of revolutions that took place across Europe in 1848, socialist revolutionaries adopted the Red Flag as a symbol of worker power. Ever since, the Red Flag has symbolised left-wing politics. Versions of it were adopted for the national flags of many communist countries during the 20th century.

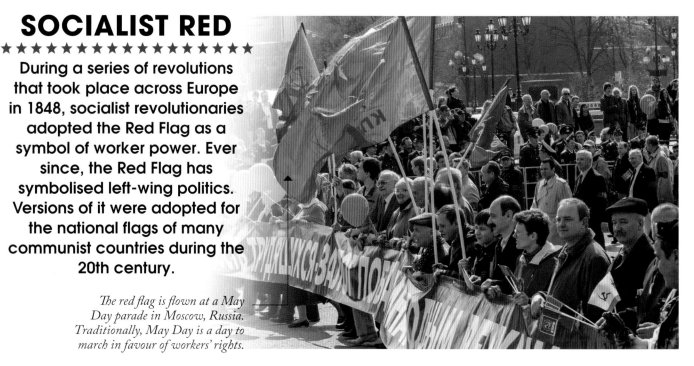

The red flag is flown at a May Day parade in Moscow, Russia. Traditionally, May Day is a day to march in favour of workers' rights.

Pride marchers in Istanbul, Turkey, carry a giant Rainbow Flag. The flag symbolises the diversity of human beings.

LGBT PRIDE

★★★★★★★★★★★★★★★★★★★★★★★★★★★★★★★★★★★★

Since the 1970s, the Rainbow Flag has been a symbol of LGBT Pride, a movement that fights for the rights of lesbian, gay, bisexual and transgender people. Designed in 1978 by San Francisco artist Gilbert Baker, the flag was first used in California. The Rainbow Flag is now often seen on LGBT Pride marches across the world. With red at the top, it shows six colours of the rainbow in order.

A flag flies from a **FLAGPOLE** outdoors, a **STAFF** indoors or a **MAST** on a ship.

FAST FLAG FACT

To mark the 25th anniversary of the Rainbow Flag, Gilbert Baker made a flag that was 2 kilometres long. It stretched across Key West, Florida, from the Atlantic Ocean to the Gulf of Mexico.

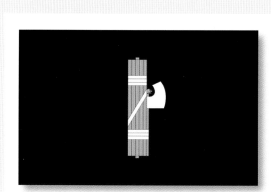

FASCIST FLAG

The right-wing National Fascist Party of Italian dictator Benito Mussolini came to power in 1922. Its flag drew on symbolism from ancient times. It depicts a *fasces*, or bundle of wooden rods, a symbol of the power of the law in ancient Rome. The Fascists wanted to create a new Italian empire to match that of Rome.

ANARCHIST FLAG

★★★★★★★★★★★★★★★★★★★★★★★★★★★★★

Anarchist groups campaign for an end to the nation state, and use a variety of flags. In the 19th century, anarchists started using black flags to symbolise the absence of the nation. Later, some groups adopted a flag that was half-red and half-black to show their socialist ideals. More recently, green anarchists have used a flag that is half-green and half-black. They campaign for an end to industrialised society.

The red half symbolises socialism.

The black half symbolises the end of the nation state.

TURKEY

The Republic of Turkey was formed in 1923 out of the old Ottoman Empire. The new republic adopted the old Ottoman flag as its new national flag.

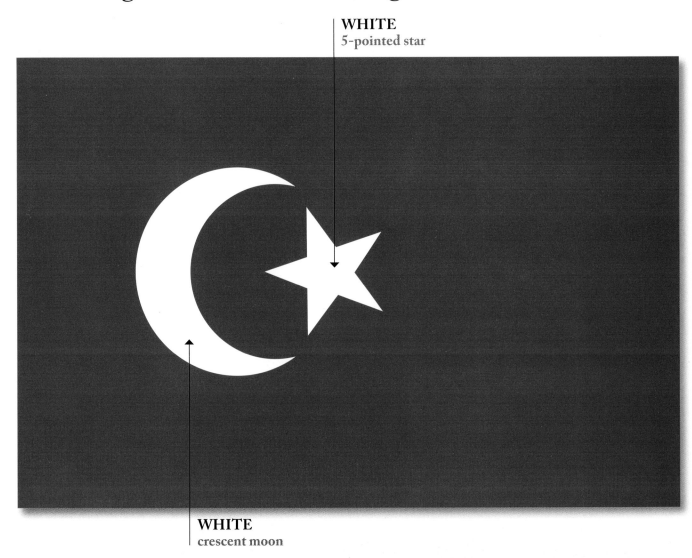

WHITE
5-pointed star

WHITE
crescent moon

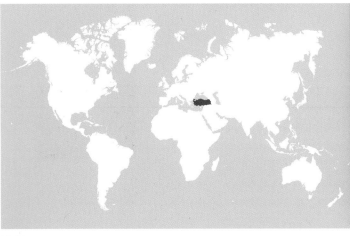

NAME:
Moon Star, or the Red Banner

DESIGN:
A white crescent moon and a white star on a red field. The design was first adopted as the official flag by the Ottomans in 1844.

OTTOMAN RULE

The city of Istanbul was captured by the Ottomans in 1453 and made the capital of their empire. The Ottoman sultans (rulers) lived in splendour in Istanbul at the Topkapi Palace, overlooking the Bosphorus strait. Like its capital city, the Ottoman Empire extended east into Asia and west into Europe. In 1923, the capital of the new Republic of Turkey was transferred to Ankara farther east, but Istanbul is still the largest city.

STAR AND CRESCENT

In the 19th century, the Ottomans ruled a powerful empire, and the star and crescent on their flag became symbols of their religion, Islam. However, the symbols first appeared more than 500 years before Islam, appearing on coins from Byzantium (an old name for Istanbul) as early as the first century CE. Most Turks are Muslim, but the modern state is secular, meaning that there is no official religion.

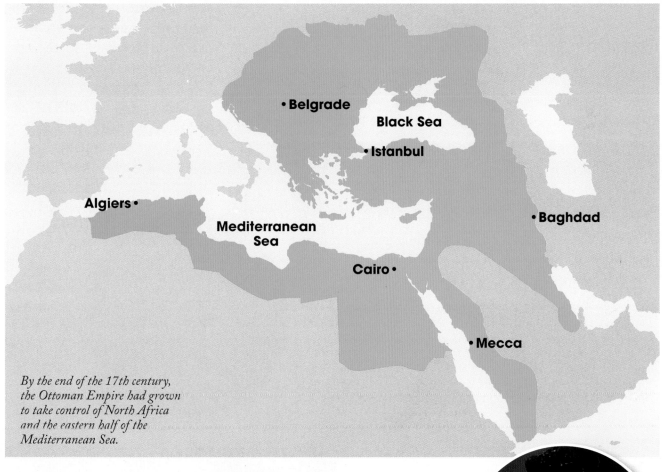

• Belgrade

Black Sea

• Istanbul

Algiers •

Mediterranean Sea

• Baghdad

Cairo •

• Mecca

By the end of the 17th century, the Ottoman Empire had grown to take control of North Africa and the eastern half of the Mediterranean Sea.

The loosely woven fabric used to make flags is called **BUNTING**.

FATHER OF MODERN TURKEY

The first president of the Republic of Turkey, Mustafa Kemal Ataturk, is widely regarded as the founding father of modern Turkey. Images of Ataturk regularly appear on flags, and there are many statues in his honour.

LEBANON

Lebanon adopted its current flag shortly before the country declared its independence from France in 1943. It features a green tree on a white and red background.

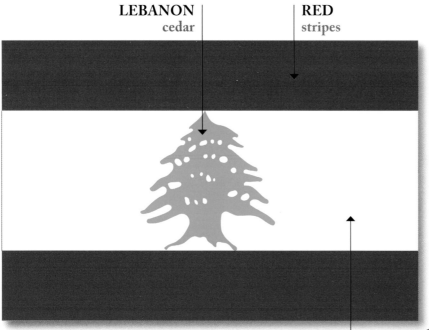

LEBANON cedar

RED stripes

WHITE
represents snow-capped mountains

LEBANON CEDAR

The Lebanon cedar is a tree that once grew widely in the mountains of Lebanon. Originally a Christian symbol, the tree has been adopted by Lebanese people of all religions as a symbol of hope in their young country. Many were cut down for ship-building, and the tree was on the verge of extinction by the 20th century. It is now protected in the mountain areas.

FAST FLAG FACT

The Lebanon cedar is mentioned in the ancient Sumerian tale, *The Epic of Gilgamesh.* The cedar groves around Lebanon's mountains were said to be the home of the gods.

Lebanon cedar appears on Lebanese coins. The Arabic and French writing on the coins reflects the country's history.

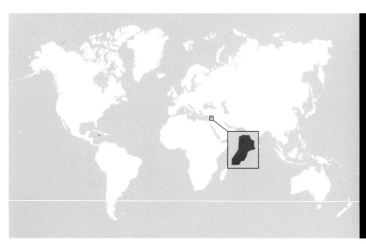

NAME:
The National Flag of Lebanon

DESIGN:
Designed by independence leader Henri Pharaon, the flag has three stripes. The white stripe is twice the width of the red stripes. The Lebanon cedar should be all green, but some flag makers give it a brown trunk.

UNITED ARAB EMIRATES

The United Arab Emirates (UAE) was formed in 1971 as a union of seven emirates, or kingdoms. Its flag is made using the pan-Arab colours, signifying Arab unity.

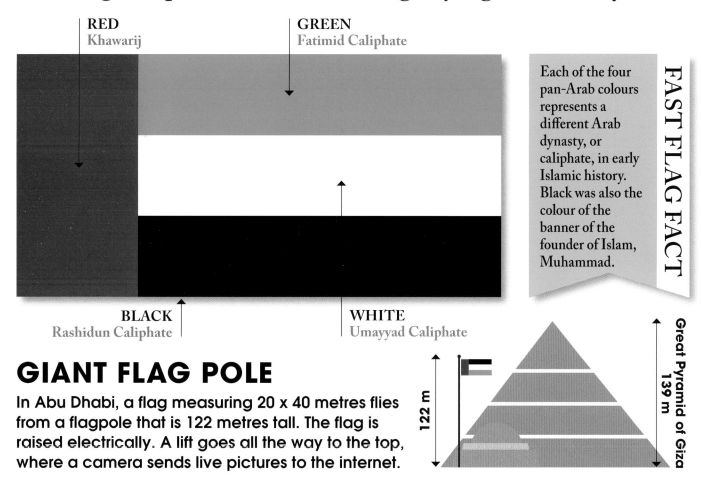

RED
Khawarij

GREEN
Fatimid Caliphate

BLACK
Rashidun Caliphate

WHITE
Umayyad Caliphate

GIANT FLAG POLE

In Abu Dhabi, a flag measuring 20 x 40 metres flies from a flagpole that is 122 metres tall. The flag is raised electrically. A lift goes all the way to the top, where a camera sends live pictures to the internet.

122 m

Great Pyramid of Giza 139 m

NAME:
The National Flag of United Arab Emirates

DESIGN:
Three equal horizontal bands of green, white and black, with a thicker vertical red band on the hoist side.

NIGERIA

With a population of more than 170 million people, Nigeria is the most populous country in Africa. Its national flag was adopted following a competition for its design held just before Nigeria became independent in 1960.

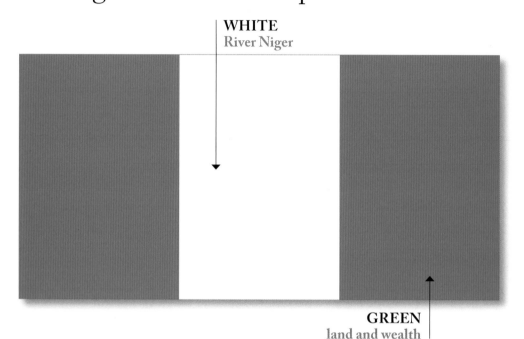

WHITE
River Niger

GREEN
land and wealth

FAST FLAG FACT

There are strict rules for the display of the flag of Nigeria. Next to a speaker on a platform, the flag should always be to the speaker's right-hand side as they face the audience.

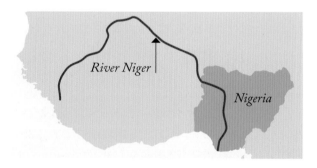

River Niger

Nigeria

RIVER AND FARMLAND

The green stripes represent Nigeria's land and natural resources. The white stripe in the centre represents the River Niger, which flows through the country from the north-west to the south, and alongside which there are large areas of lush, green farmland.

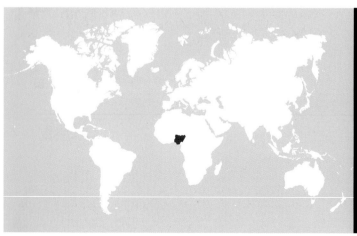

NAME:
Flag of Nigeria

DESIGN:
The flag was designed by 23-year-old student Taiwo Akinkunmi, whose flag was chosen from 3,000 entries. His original design had a red Sun at its centre, but this was later dropped.

KENYA

The flag of Kenya, adopted on independence in 1963, features the red, black and green colours of pan-African unity. The emblem is a traditional Maasai shield.

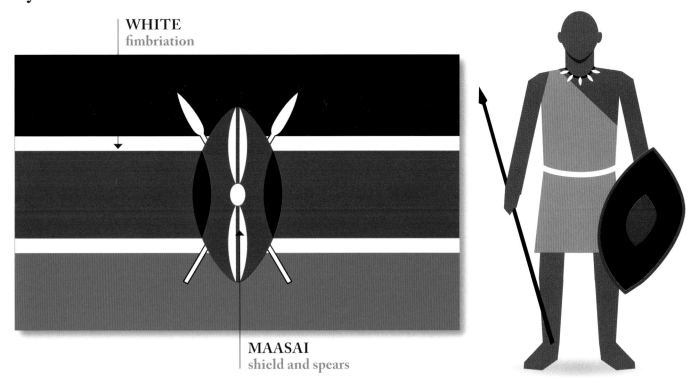

WHITE fimbriation

MAASAI shield and spears

FAST FLAG FACT

Kenya has a diverse population, and 69 different languages are spoken there. The two official languages are English and Swahili. The Swahili name for the national flag is 'Bendera'.

MAASAI WARRIORS

The Maasai are nomadic herders who range across southern Kenya and northern Tanzania. They move seasonally with their cattle, following the best grazing land. Traditionally, young Maasai men were brought up to be warriors. They gained a reputation as tall and fearless fighters.

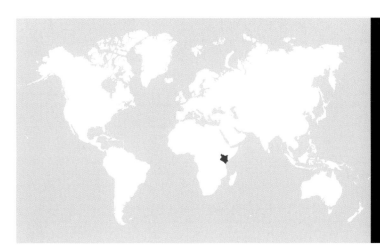

NAME:
Flag of Kenya, or Bendera

DESIGN:
Three equal horizontal bands of black, red and green, with a Maasai shield and spears at the centre. White fimbriation separates the colours. The shape is a ratio of 2:3.

SOUTH AFRICA

The South African flag was first flown on 10 May 1994, the day that Nelson Mandela was elected the first president of the new democratic state. It replaced the old flag that had come to represent the racist apartheid regime.

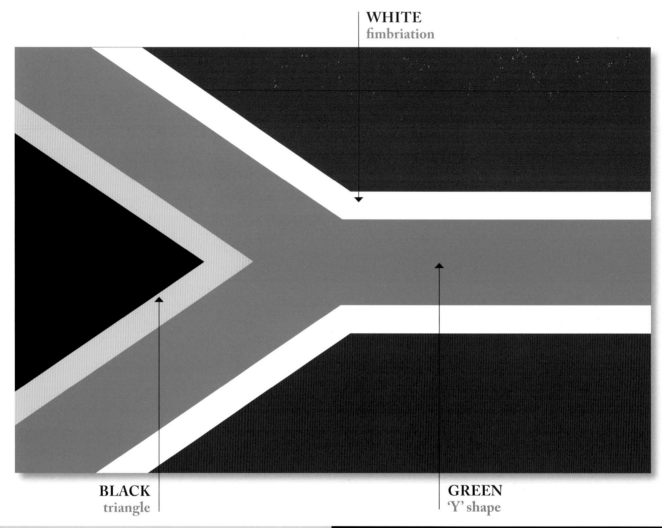

WHITE
fimbriation

BLACK
triangle

GREEN
'Y' shape

NAME:
Unofficially known as the Rainbow Flag, as it represents the diverse population of South Africa

DESIGN:
The design by Frederick Brownell includes black, green and yellow, the colours of the African National Congress. These are added to the red, white and blue colours that appeared on the old flag.

THE FIRST AFRICAN IN SPACE

In 2002, South African computer tycoon Mark Shuttleworth became the first African astronaut when he spent eight days in orbit around Earth on the International Space Station. Dubbed the 'Afronaut', Shuttleworth funded his trip himself. He spoke to former president Nelson Mandela from the space station.

Shuttleworth's logo was a space rocket in the colours of the South African flag.

APARTHEID REGIME

The flag of South Africa between 1928 and 1994 had three small flags at its centre. They represented the European colonies that united to form South Africa, eventually leading to the racist apartheid regime that separated people by skin colour. The flag was seen to exclude the black majority population, and when the apartheid regime fell, it was felt that a new, inclusive design was needed.

At the centre of the old flag were the British Union Flag and the flags of the Orange Free State and Transvaal.

ANC

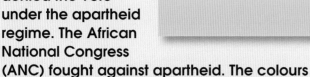

Before 1994, black South Africans were denied the vote under the apartheid regime. The African National Congress (ANC) fought against apartheid. The colours of the ANC flag were included on the new post-apartheid South African flag.

NELSON MANDELA

Nelson Mandela was an ANC leader who spent 28 years in prison. He was released in 1990, and four years later became the country's first democratically elected president as the apartheid regime was replaced. The new flag was rushed into production to be ready for Mandela's inauguration as president.

Nelson Mandela stands next to his daughter Zinani while he is sowrn in as president in 1994.

Algeria's national flag was first officially flown in 1962, when the country gained independence from France. It had previously been used by the Algerian Liberation Front, the group that fought for independence.

GREEN
symbolises Islam

WHITE
symbolises purity

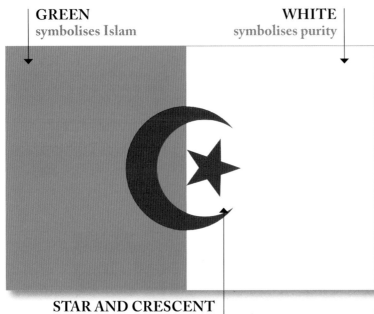

STAR AND CRESCENT
reflect Ottoman past

The side of a flag from which it is meant to be viewed is called its **OBVERSE** side.

OTTOMAN RULE

From 1525 to 1830, Algeria was ruled by the Ottomans. They used the city of Algiers as a base from which to control North Africa and attack Europe. In 1830, the French invaded and took over.

FAST FLAG FACT

Algeria has strict laws forbidding its citizens from insulting the flag. In 2010, 17 people were sent to prison for disrespecting the flag at a political protest.

During the 18th century, the ensign of the Ottoman Empire flew from ships leaving Algiers.

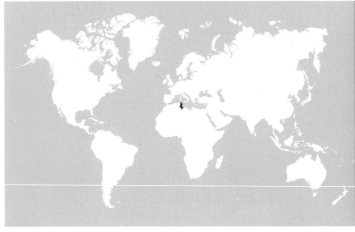

NAME:
Flag of the Democratic and Popular Republic of Algeria

DESIGN:
A red star and crescent on a background that is half green and half red. The star and crescent reflect the 300 years that Algeria spent as part of the Ottoman Empire before French rule. The flag has a proportion of 2:3.

ETHIOPIA

The red, green and yellow flag was first used by the Ethiopian Empire in 1897, celebrating the successful defence of the country against invading Italians.

YELLOW
central band

GREEN
top band

RED
bottom band

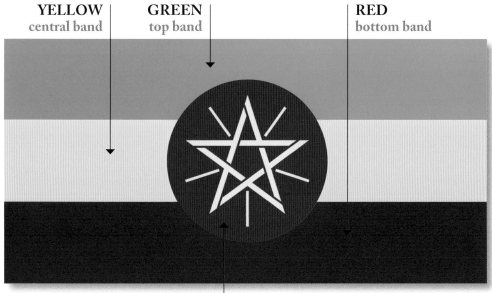

NATIONAL EMBLEM
of Ethiopia

ERITREA

Eritrea became independent from Ethiopia in 1993 following a long civil war. The country's name is taken from the Greek word for the Red Sea, along which it sits. Eritrea has been involved in a series of conflicts since independence.

Yellow olive wreath on the flag of Eritrea symbolises the hope for peace.

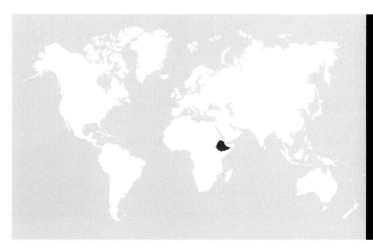

NAME:
Flag of Ethiopia

DESIGN:
Three equal horizontal bands of green, yellow and red. The emblem was given its current form in 1996, on a large dark blue disc. The pentagram (five-pointed star) symbolises the unity of the people.

WARNING FLAGS

Flags are often used to give warnings. These flags can be seen from long distances and understood by everyone, whatever language they speak. Red is often chosen for the greatest danger, as this colour attracts immediate attention.

ICS
North America

ALPHA
Europe

DIVER DOWN

★★★

When scuba divers are underwater, a flag is placed on a buoy or a boat where they entered the water. The flag warns other boats to keep away to avoid the chance of hitting the divers. The red and white 'ICS' design used in North America was introduced by US Naval diver Denzel James Dockery in 1956. In Europe, the international maritime signal flag 'alpha' is used to give the same warning.

LIVE FIRING

★★★★★★★★★★★★★★★★★★★★★★★★★★★★

Armies often use remote parts of the countryside as ranges to practise live firing. The danger areas are clearly marked, and red flags are raised to warn walkers when an exercise is in progress. Red lamps are used at night.

COASTGUARD FLAG

★★★★★★★★★★★★★★★★★★★★★★★★★

On beaches, coastguards use a system of flags to tell bathers where it is safe to swim. Boards at the beach explain the meaning of each flag.

Red flag
No swimming at all

Between two red and yellow flags
Safe to swim and belly board

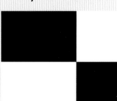

Between two black and white flags
No swimming – area used by surfers and windsurfers

SHARK!

In Cape Town, South Africa, sharks are a threat to swimmers. Warning flags indicate the level of danger.

Spotting conditions are good, and no sharks have been seen.

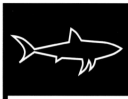

Spotting conditions are bad, but no sharks have been seen.

Shark alert! Sharks have been spotted.

Get out of the water now! This flag is accompanied by a loud siren.

SAILORS BEWARE

★★★★★★★★★★★★★

In the 18th century, pirate ships would raise a flag called the Jolly Roger when they were about to attack another ship. The design of a skull with two long bones underneath it was intended to strike fear into the sailors on the ship they were attacking.

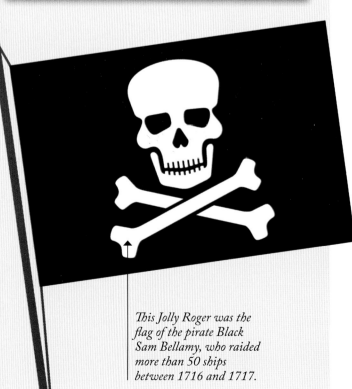

This Jolly Roger was the flag of the pirate Black Sam Bellamy, who raided more than 50 ships between 1716 and 1717.

CHINA

The flag of the People's Republic of China was adopted as the national flag in 1949, shortly after the Communist Party had come to power at the end of a long civil war.

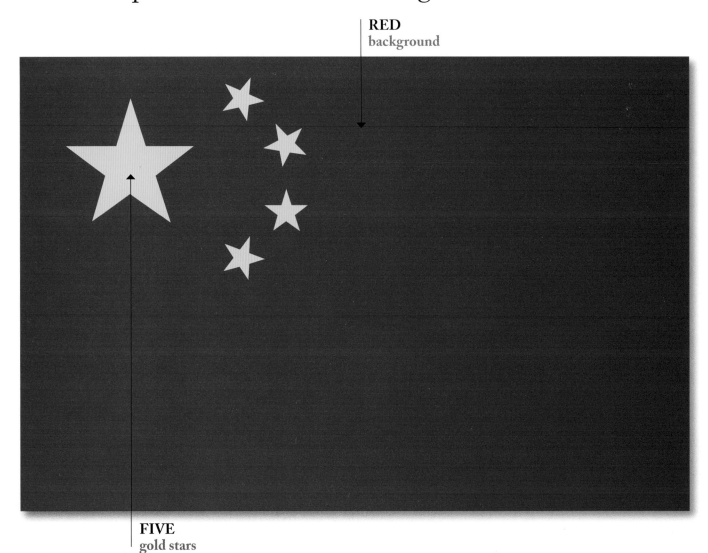

RED
background

FIVE
gold stars

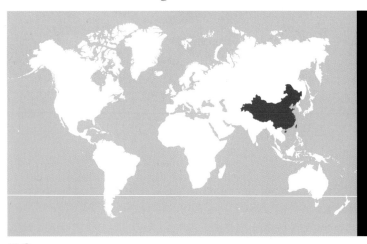

NAME:
The Five-Star Red Flag

DESIGN:
A red flag with five gold stars in the upper hoist-side canton. There is one large star with four smaller ones to its left arranged in a semi-circle. It was designed by economist Zeng Liansong in 1949.

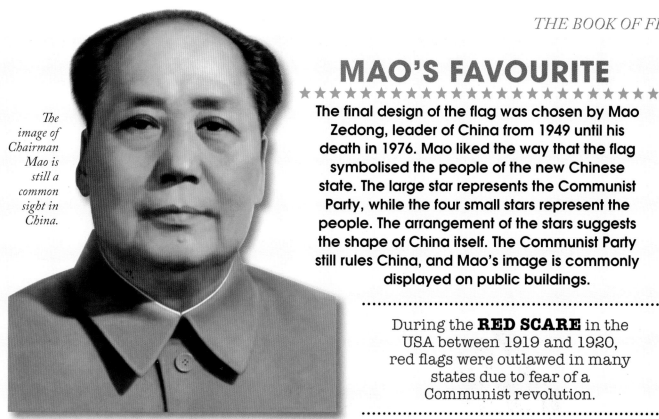

The image of Chairman Mao is still a common sight in China.

MAO'S FAVOURITE

The final design of the flag was chosen by Mao Zedong, leader of China from 1949 until his death in 1976. Mao liked the way that the flag symbolised the people of the new Chinese state. The large star represents the Communist Party, while the four small stars represent the people. The arrangement of the stars suggests the shape of China itself. The Communist Party still rules China, and Mao's image is commonly displayed on public buildings.

During the **RED SCARE** in the USA between 1919 and 1920, red flags were outlawed in many states due to fear of a Communist revolution.

AUTONOMOUS AREAS

The two former European colonies Hong Kong and Macau are the only places in China that are allowed their own flags. These so-called 'special administrative regions' have separate political and legal systems and maintain a large amount of independence from the rest of China. Both flags include the five stars of the Chinese flag in their designs.

Macau
The flag of Macau shows a lotus flower over a bridge. The bridge represents Macau's importance as a major port. A former Portuguese colony, Macau joined China in 1999.

Hong Kong
The flag of Hong Kong shows an orchid flower. The Hong Kong orchid tree was discovered in Hong Kong in 1880 and has become a symbol of the city. A former British colony, Hong Kong joined China in 1997.

TAIWAN

In 1950, the Chinese Civil War ended in victory for the Communist forces of Mao Zedong. The defeated Nationalists led by Chiang Kai-shek fled to the island of Taiwan, where they set up a rival Chinese state. Taiwan remains an independent state, and still uses the old flag of the Republic of China, which shows a white Sun on a blue background in the hoist canton, with a red background.

SOUTH KOREA

The national flag of the Republic of Korea (South Korea) was adopted in 1950, two years after Korea was divided into two countries following World War II. It is a new version of an old symbol representing harmony in the world.

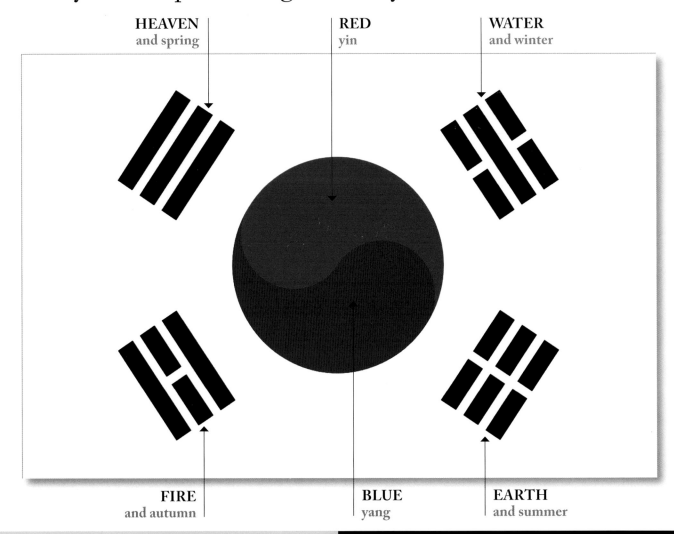

HEAVEN
and spring

RED
yin

WATER
and winter

FIRE
and autumn

BLUE
yang

EARTH
and summer

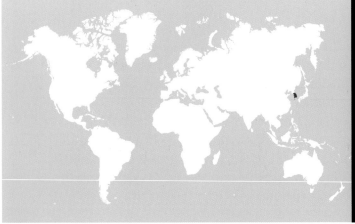

NAME:
The Taegeuki (the flag of the taegeuk)

DESIGN:
At the centre is the *taegeuk*, or yin-yang, symbol. Surrounding this are four groups of long and short black bars, called kwae. The kwae represent heaven, earth, fire and water, and are arranged in a way that provides balance between opposites. The kwae also represent the four seasons.

OPPOSITES AND HARMONY

The symbol at the centre of the flag, called a *taegeuk* in Korean, is more commonly known in English as yin-yang. The symbol first appeared in Korea more than 1,000 years ago, and it reflects the influence of Taoism in the peninsula. In Taoist thought, yin and yang are two opposites that form a whole, and these opposites wrap around each other in the *taegeuk* to represent harmony.

South Korean guards face their North Korean counterparts across the border.

JOSEON KINGDOM

Between the 14th and 19th centuries, Korea was a united Kingdom ruled by the Joseon dynasty. Many grand temples were built in this period, as the arts and sciences flourished. The royal standard of the Joseon period features eight kwae. Four of these were chosen for the flag of South Korea.

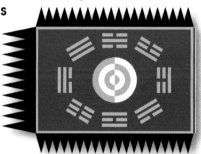

This design for the royal standard dates from 1800.

DIVIDING LINE

North and South Korea are divided at the 38th parallel line of latitude. The border is 250 kilometres long. All the way along the border, troops from North and South face one another across an area 4 kilometres wide called the Demilitarised Zone. It is the most heavily guarded border in the world.

NORTH KOREA

Officially called the Democratic People's Republic of Korea, North Korea is almost totally closed to the outside world. Its flag features a red star to symbolise communism. North Korea's communist regime has been guilty of human rights abuses, and the standard of living is very low. Tensions with South Korea remain high.

JAPAN

A design showing a large red Sun was first used officially as the flag of Japan in 1854, and was formally made the national flag in 1999. The symbol of the Sun has been associated with Japan for more than 1,000 years.

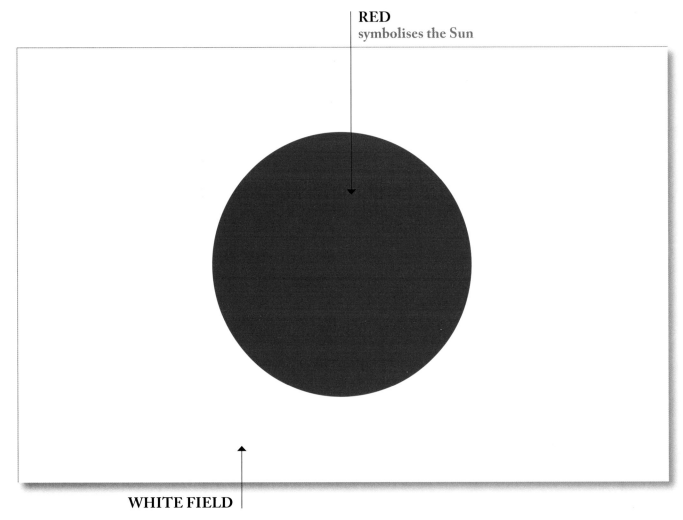

RED
symbolises the Sun

WHITE FIELD

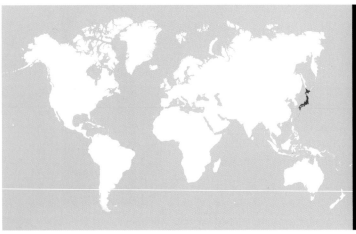

NAME:
Officially called Nisshoki (the Sun flag), but more commonly known as Hinomaru (the circle of the Sun).

DESIGN:
A white field with a red disk in its centre, representing the Sun at dawn.

LAND OF THE RISING SUN

★★★

Japan is a group of islands to the east of the continent of Asia. The ancient Japanese did not know of any land farther east, so they believed that their islands were the first to be greeted by the Sun as it rose in the east each morning. The Japanese word for Japan is Nippon, which means 'Land of the Rising Sun'. The red disk on the flag represents the Sun at dawn.

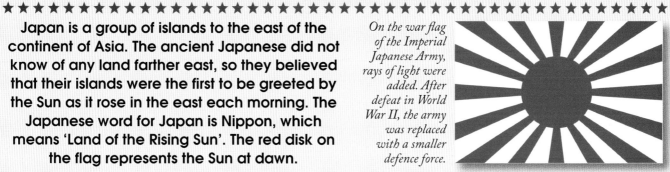

On the war flag of the Imperial Japanese Army, rays of light were added. After defeat in World War II, the army was replaced with a smaller defence force.

GOOD LUCK FLAG

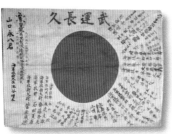

During World War II, soldiers going off to fight would carry a Japanese flag with them. This flag was known as a Yosegaki Hinomaru, or Good Luck Flag. Friends and family would write messages and poems of support on the flag, and sometimes they would dip their hands in ink and leave hand prints. The soldiers carried the flags under their clothing when they went into battle.

FAST FLAG FACT

The first recorded use of a flag representing the Sun dates from the 8th century. The ancient history book *Shoki Nihongi*, written in 797, says that the Emperor Mommu used one at his court in 701.

The flag of **NEPAL** is the only national flag that is not rectangular. Its shape was made by combining two triangular pennants.

SAMURAI

In the 15th and 16th centuries, before Japan was unified under one leader, rival regional lords would battle against one another. Each lord had his own flag. Their elite soldiers, known as samurai, would ride into battle with the flag of their lord on their backs to identify which side they were fighting for.

The samurai were a class of highly trained warriors. They were particularly famed for their skilled swordsmanship.

THAILAND

The Thai flag, made up of five horizontal stripes, dates from 1917. Several different versions had been used before this simplified form was agreed upon.

BLUE BAND
represents the Thai royal family

RED BANDS
represent the people

ELEPHANT FLAG

The first flag of Thailand was created in 1855. It featured a white elephant, which was a royal symbol. The elephant was removed from the flag in 1917 on the order of King Vajiravudh. It is said that the king was angered when he saw the flag flying upside-down, and decided to replace the design with a symmetrical one that looks the same either way up.

FAST FLAG FACT

The Thai king Bhumibol Adulyadej came to the throne in 1946, and is the world's longest-serving ruler. He has his own flag, which features a Garuda, a mythical half-man, half-bird creature.

White elephants are considered sacred in Thailand. Historically, they have been given as presents to Thai kings.

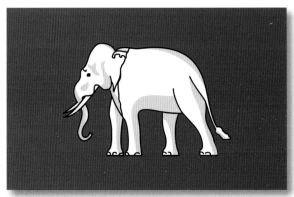

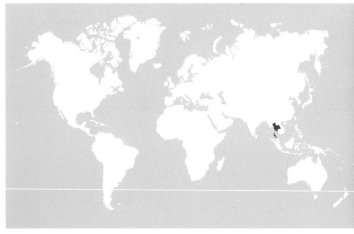

NAME:
Thong Trairong, meaning the 'three-colour flag'

DESIGN:
Five horizontal stripes, with red top and bottom, white stripes next to the red, and a thicker blue stripe in the centre. The central blue stripe fills one-third of the flag, while each of the other four stripes fills one-sixth.

INDONESIA

The flag of the Republic of Indonesia has a simple design. It has been the national flag of the country ever since the declaration of independence in 1945. Indonesia became officially independent from the Netherlands in 1950.

RED
top half

WHITE
bottom half

SPICE ISLANDS

Between 1800 and 1945, the country was ruled by the Dutch and known as the Dutch East Indies. The colony was a source of wealth for the Netherlands, which exported its valuable spices to the rest of the world.

Indonesia's warm, wet climate and rich volcanic soils make it an ideal place to grow many kinds of spices.

If you turn the Indonesian flag upside down, it becomes the **POLISH** flag.

NAME:
Sang Merah-Putih (The Red-and-White)

DESIGN:
The simple two-colour design uses the same colours as the emblem of the Majapahit Empire, which ruled much of Southeast Asia between the 13th and 15th centuries, and was centred on the Indonesian island of Java.

INDIA

The largest democratic country in the world, with 1.2 billion citizens, India adopted its national flag on winning independence from the UK in 1947.

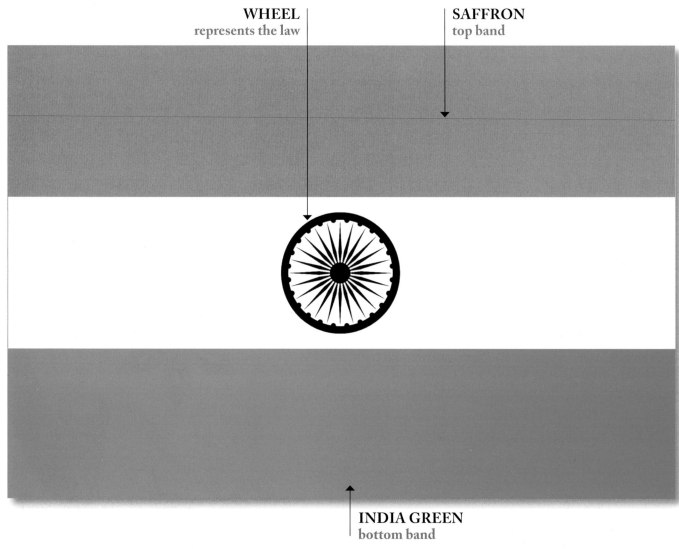

WHEEL
represents the law

SAFFRON
top band

INDIA GREEN
bottom band

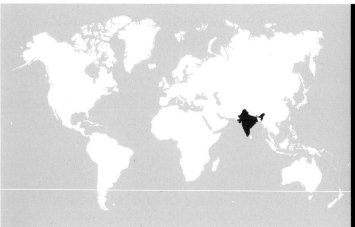

NAME:
Tiranga (tricolour)

DESIGN:
The design, by independence fighter Pingali Venkayya, has three equal bands of saffron, white and India green. In the centre is a navy blue wheel with 24 spokes, representing a *dharmachakra* (wheel of the law).

Four Lions stand on top of the Lion Capital, facing north, south, east and west.

FAST FLAG FACT

On 7 December 2014, more than 50,000 Indians came together in the YMCA grounds in Chennai to form the world's largest human flag. Each person held up a coloured card to form their small part of the flag, which was filmed from the air to mark the event.

WHEEL OF THE LAW

The national emblem of India is called the Ashoka Chakra. It is named after the ancient Indian Mauryan emperor Ashoka the Great, who ruled in the third century BCE. Ashoka built the Lion Capital sculpture at Sarnath, the site of the Buddha's first sermon and a sacred place for Buddhists. The Capital features the design of a wheel with 24 spokes, also called a *dharmachakra* (wheel of the law), which represents the teachings of the Buddha.

The Ashoka Chakra, or dharmachakra, appears at the bottom.

PAKISTAN

When India won independence, it was split into two countries – India and Pakistan. Pakistan adopted a green flag with a star and crescent to symbolise its majority-Muslim population. The white band on the hoist side represents religious minorities.

INCLUSIVE FLAG

★★★★★★★★★★★★★★★★★★★★★★★★★★

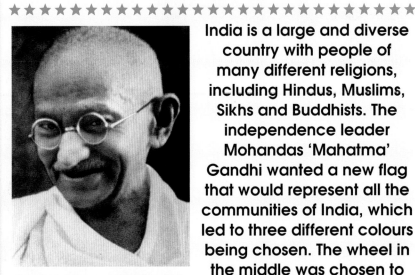

Gandhi led a campaign of peaceful resistance. He was given the name 'Mahatma', meaning 'Great Soul'.

India is a large and diverse country with people of many different religions, including Hindus, Muslims, Sikhs and Buddhists. The independence leader Mohandas 'Mahatma' Gandhi wanted a new flag that would represent all the communities of India, which led to three different colours being chosen. The wheel in the middle was chosen to represent the health and prosperity of the nation.

AUSTRALIA

Australia's flag features the Union Flag in the upper hoist-side canton, which shows that the British queen or king is the country's monarch. The flag was officially adopted in 1908.

UNION FLAG

STAR
represents Commonwealth

STAR CONSTELLATION
represents Southern Cross

The **ABORIGINAL** flag, which represents the country's first inhabitants, is an official flag of Australia.

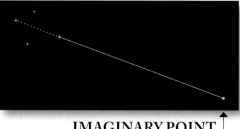

IMAGINARY POINT
above due south

THE SOUTHERN CROSS

Crux, or the Southern Cross, is the smallest of the 88 constellations. It is easily visible from the southern hemisphere, where sailors use it for navigation. A line drawn from the top of the cross to the bottom, then extended 4.5 times, points to a place in the sky that is directly above due south.

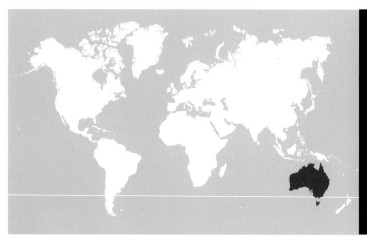

NAME:
Australian National Flag

DESIGN:
Five white stars of the Southern Cross constellation plus the seven-pointed Commonwealth Star on a blue background. The Union Flag is in the upper-hoist canton.

NEW ZEALAND

New Zealand's flag also shows the Southern Cross. Similar in design to Australia's flag, but with just the four main stars of the constellation, it was first used in 1869, and adopted officially in 1902.

UNION FLAG

STAR CONSTELLATION
represents Southern Cross

A NEW FLAG?

In 2014, the government announced plans to ask the people of New Zealand whether they want a new flag. A leading alternative is the Silver Fern flag, which is already used unofficially as a symbol of New Zealand by the national cricket and rugby teams. The silver fern is a large tree fern that is only found in New Zealand.

FAST FLAG FACT

In 2010, the National Maori flag was flown for the first time on official buildings next to the New Zealand flag. The Maori were the first people to settle in New Zealand.

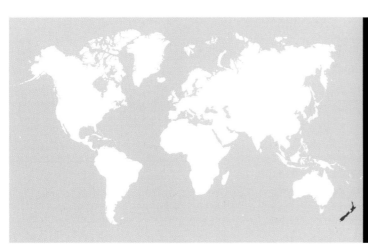

NAME:
The national flag of New Zealand

DESIGN:
Four red stars with white borders on a blue background, with a Union Flag in the upper-hoist canton.

SPORTS FLAGS

In many sports, referees use flags to signal to the players, the crowd or each other when play needs to be halted. In martial arts contests, judges use flags to show who has won.

FORMULA 1

In Formula 1 racing, the marshals by the side of the track communicate with the drivers using a variety of flags. There are ten flags in all, some giving instructions to drivers, others giving warnings:

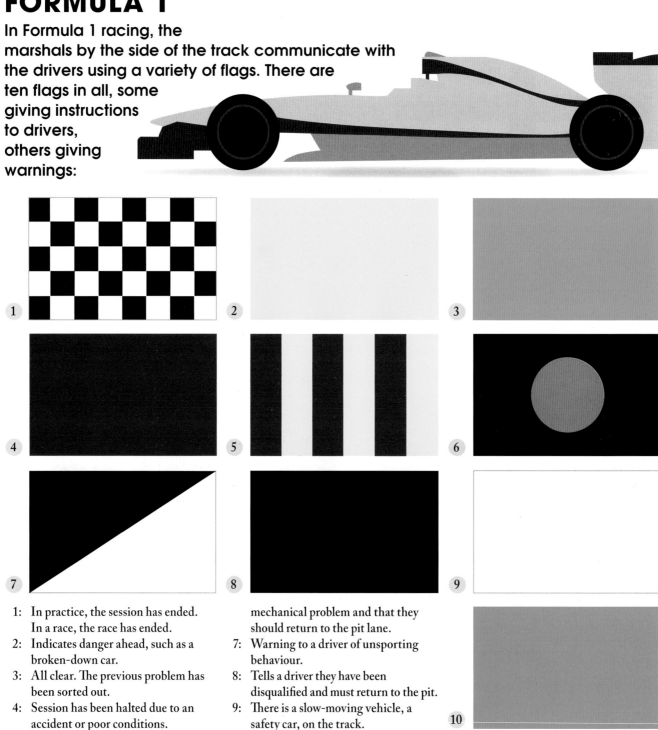

1: In practice, the session has ended. In a race, the race has ended.

2: Indicates danger ahead, such as a broken-down car.

3: All clear. The previous problem has been sorted out.

4: Session has been halted due to an accident or poor conditions.

5: Slippery track, due to water or oil.

6: Warns a driver that the car has a mechanical problem and that they should return to the pit lane.

7: Warning to a driver of unsporting behaviour.

8: Tells a driver they have been disqualified and must return to the pit.

9: There is a slow-moving vehicle, a safety car, on the track.

10: Tells a driver that a car is behind and that he must allow it to overtake.

FOOTBALL

★★★★★★★★★★★★★★★★★★★★★★★★★★★★

During a football match, two assistant referees run along the side of the pitch. Each assistant carries a flag, and uses it to signal to the referee to stop play because a player is offside, the ball has gone out for a throw-in or a player is to be substituted.

The assistant referees need to be fit, as they must run to stay level with the last line of one team's defence. This allows them to judge when a player from the other team is offside.

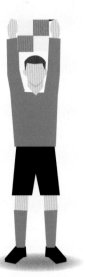

Throw-in   **Substitution**   **Offside**

FAST FLAG FACTS

In American football, officials use yellow flags to indicate penalties. The flags are not attached to poles, but instead are pieces of weighted cloth. When a referee spots an infringement of the rules, he or she throws the flag onto the field of play to show where the penalty should take place.

In ski races, competitors must pass through gates marked by pairs of poles with flags on them. They alternately pass through pairs of red flags and blue flags. In slalom races, the gates are placed close together. If a skier misses out any of the gates, they are disqualified from the race.

Red flag is held in right hand.

White flag in left hand.

KENDO

In many martial arts, such as kendo, the judges hold a flag in each hand. One competitor is represented by a red flag, and the other by a white one. At the end of the contest, the head judge raises one of the flags to indicate the winner.

GLOSSARY

autonomous
Enjoying some independence from central government.

canton
A quarter of a flag, particularly the upper hoist quarter.

coat of arms
A design on the shield of a medieval knight.

colony
A country that is controlled and settled by another country.

ensign
A flag flown by a ship.

field
The background colour of a flag.

fimbriation
A narrow line on a flag that makes its design clearer.

fly
The side of a flag farthest from the flag pole.

hectare
A unit of measurement for area. One hectare equals 10,000 m^2.

hoist
The side of a flag closest to the flag pole.

monarchy
A system of government with a king or queen as its head of state.

nationalism
A political movement that wishes to create or strengthen a nation.

nomadic
With no fixed home.

republic
A system of government with a president as its head of state.

standard
A ceremonial flag, often carried by an army.

INDEX